Italian

Learn Italian for Beginners: A Simple Guide that Will Help You on Your Language Learning Journey

Contents

Introduction

The fourth most studied language in the world, according to the General Assembly of the Italian Language in the World, is, in fact, Italian.

It is surprising to discover that the language of a very small Mediterranean peninsula can compete with much more widespread ones. With over two million scholars each year, Italian exceeds French, despite the spread of this latter language in Africa and North America.

Why? There are many reasons behind the decision to learn Italian: from having Italian relatives to wanting to travel to one of the most beautiful countries in the world. However, there is no need to make hypotheses—if you are reading this introduction, you have been led here by your desire to learn this language.

The purpose of this book is to present itself as the best solution for those approaching Italian for the first time. This is not a booklet with a handful of sentences already built or a two-thousand-page manual on how to become a Neo-Latin linguist.

What the next few pages lay out is the groundwork for proper communication in Italian. You will see the construction of sentences, the use of accents, and then the most common expressions of this idiom.

Italian is a musical language, beautiful to hear and speak, but very difficult to master. This is why you will take small steps, moving forward only once a concept is fully understood.

You will start with the pronouns, singular and plural, and discover the first differences that run between English and Italian.

At this point, the book will focus on verbs, to explain and analyze all the elements that are part of a sentence, before discovering the most common sentences used in Italian.

This way, the language you will learn will be the one used every day, which will allow you to move freely around the Italian streets and get to know the uses and customs of Italian.

You will see how to present yourself, friends, and family, talk about school and work, enjoy art and food, and get to the most common questions that every aspiring Italian speaker asks.

This manual will cover everything you need to know to take your first steps in Italy. For this reason, much of the book is dedicated to the Italian culture. This is because it is essential to understand the people behind a language in order to love it even more and fully understand it. Knowing the culture will allow you to develop more conversational Italian, as well as having all the information you need if you ever decide to travel to Italy.

The book is divided into three major sections.

The first section is dedicated to Italian grammar, which is necessary to understand how to construct and understand a sentence.

The second section is dedicated to traveling in Italy, including information and essential phrases. This section is not only meant for those who want to visit this country, but also for those who want to know all the most common phrases to be exchanged with people who do not know each other.

Finally, the third section proposes an in-depth study dedicated to those who are thinking of moving to Italy, an overview of Italian culture, further education on the Italian people, and more everyday phrases.

Based on this, you might regard this book as a training course in which to learn Italian from every point of view, to fully understand it and speed up your learning process.

So, without further ado, let's start by talking about the construction of the sentence.

Pronouns... single, plural, formal, and informal.

The grammatical aspect is the most technical and tedious to deal with when learning a new language. Despite this, you need to understand the functioning of Italian sentences.

Once you understand the behavior of the two main elements of each sentence, the pronoun and the verb, you can move among the common phrases of this language.

Speaking of pronouns, right from the start, you will begin to notice the profound differences between English and Italian. For this reason, take your time and read the first chapter carefully.

Before moving on to the analysis of every type of pronoun, it is necessary to take a small step back to understand the sentences that are later used as examples.

Pronunciation

Pronunciation is usually a more advanced topic while learning a different language, especially in a guide based on learning the most common sentences that help to be an active part of an Italian conversation.

For this reason, the pronunciation is often proposed at the final phase of a guide, but this book teaches it in the early chapters to allow you to improve much more.

If pronunciation was delegated to the last part of the book, readers could have some difficulties not only with reading the sentences in the guide, but they also might not be able to correct their potential pronunciation mistakes.

Thus, all the technical parts are within the early chapters, so you can understand both Italian sentence structure and how sentences and words are pronounced.

You will find that repeating words while proceeding will improve your pronunciation by the end of the guide.

It is also encouraged that you be patient and begin your journey into the Italian language by starting with the single letters.

Despite the rules, always remember that the phonetics in Italian is much simpler than you think. This is because Italian words are almost always read as they are written. For this reason, once you learn the basic rules of various letters' pronunciation, you will discover that learning to pronounce words is suitable for all. Moreover, once you learn the first words, others will follow the same examples, creating an exponentially faster improvement process.

The Vowels

Let's start with the vowels since the consonants have a similar pronunciation to the English ones (with few exceptions). The Italian vowels are five:

A   E   I   O   U

Below is the pronunciation of each vowel:

A

The **A**'s pronunciation is the same as the U in the English word "**Cut**". Luckily, the pronunciation remains the same, so once you have practiced the form, you can repeat it on every word that includes it.

E

E shows itself in different forms. Mainly the Italian **E** has two sounds based on the accent mark (visible or not) on it, which tends to be confused, even by Italians based on their regional background.

This different explanation is important as with a different accent mark on it, the whole meaning of the word could change. For example:

Pèsca – Peach

Pésca – To fish

This is a subtle nuance you will learn with time and experience, mostly because the accent marks in the examples are not visible in the written language. These are shown only when the accent marks fall on the last letter of the word.

So, how is the letter **E** pronounced?

The open E, as for "Pèsca", is pronounced similarly to the E of the English word "rest". While the closed E of "Pésca" (to fish) is similar to the E of the English word "appointment".

As previously mentioned, there is no way of knowing when to use the open or closed E—unless you have experience with the language. You may find the E with an accent mark, but only when it is the only one or at the end of a word.

For example:

Lui **è** bello – He is handsome

Perché l'ho detto io – Because I said so.

In these cases, remember that "è" is pronounced as "rest" and "é" is pronounced as "appointment".

I

I is one of the vowels that sound different from the English language. The pronunciation of I in Italian is similar to the **Y** in English, like in the word "baby" or even the double **EE** as in the word "meet".

O

O has two distinct pronunciations based on the hidden accent, so much that in many Italian regions, they are used incorrectly.

The pronunciation of **O** is similar to the English word "dog", but it can also sound closed, such as the English word "post".

U

U is similar to the double **OO** in English, like for the word "doom" or even the same **U** in the word "loud".

By knowing the pronunciation of the vowels, you can pronounce most Italian words correctly. There are some special cases concerning the consonants, which you will see in the next section of this chapter.

Consonants

Most of the Italian consonants, as mentioned, have a pronunciation similar to the English ones, which will be convenient when learning this language.

However, there are exceptions.

C

In Italian, **C** has two different pronunciations: one is soft, and the other is hard, with both based on the letter that follows.

If the vowel **I** or **E** follows the letter C, then it will have a soft sound, similar to the English word "chilly". If instead it is followed by any other letter, **C** will have a hard sound, similar to the English word "cat".

Note: if the letter C is followed by the letter **H** and then by an **I** and **E**, it will still sound hard, such as in the English word "cat".

For example:

Ciao (Hi) – soft sound

Chiesa (Church) – hard sound

G

G follows the same rules as **C**: it has a soft sound in the presence of the letter **I** or **E** (similar to the English word "June") and a hard sound with other letters (similar to the English word "Gift").

If an **L** follows the **G** and then an **I** or **E**, it will have a very particular sound, almost non-existent in the English language. The closest word to that could be "million" with the double **LL**, but the sound is still slightly different.

Remember: there are irregular words that maintain a hard pronunciation (as in the English word "Glimpse"), even in the presence of these vowels, such as "Glicemia" (Glycemia)—although these are very rare.

Another very common combination of the letter G is the one created with the consonant N. GN has a particular sound that can also be found in the Spanish ñ. This construction is found in words like:

Signore – Mister

H

H is mute and used to make other consonants hard (**C** or **G,** as you have seen before) or is not pronounced at all.

Example: the word "hotel", in Italian, is pronounced as if the H was not present.

Q

Q is not used so much in the Italian language, although it is part of important words, such as "acqua" (water). Usually, it is also accompanied by the letter **C**, for all those words that descend from the word "acqua", such as:

Acquitrino – Marsh

Acquario – Aquarium

However, it can be found even as a single letter in words like:

Quadro – Painting

Fortunately, in both cases, this letter's pronunciation remains the same, which is very similar to the English letter **K**, with a hard pronunciation, such as the letter **C**.

S

The **SC** couple can have a soft or hard sound too. It follows the same rules as **C**, and the soft sound occurs only if it is followed by an **I** or **E**. In this case, it has a pronunciation similar to the English **SH** (shoe). Some examples:

Pro**sci**utto – Ham

Scelta – Choice

While, in any other case, they have a hard sound, like the English word "task", here are some examples:

Mo**sca** – Fly

Scarpa – Shoe

As in the case of the **C**, if an **H** and the vowels follow the **SC**, the sound still remains hard:

Schiena – Back

Furthermore, the letter **S** is one of those consonants that has a double sound in the Italian language. It can come closer to the letter **Z** sound, as in the English word "zebra", or even have a much sweeter sound, like the letter **S** of the English word "still".

The following are some examples of words that contain the **S** and how its sound may change from word to word:

Casa (*House*) – Hard sound, **Z**

Borsa (*Bag*) – Soft sound, **S**

Studiare (*To study*) – Soft sound, **S**

Rosa (*Rose*) – Hard sound, **Z**

How to know when one sound should be used rather than another? Unfortunately, even in this case, as in other phases of this manual, only experience can help you, and the more you speak the language, the more you will realize when to use a certain pronunciation.

Overall, the letter **S** is often pronounced with the soft sound of "still", but there is a large number of words in Italian in which the pronunciation has a much harder sound.

Z

Z is also pronounced differently based on its position within a word.

When **Z** is at the beginning of a word, it acquires a hard, buzzing-like sound, like the one of the letter **S** but even more distinct. You can see it in words like:

Zucchero (Sugar)

Zaino (Backpack)

However, it can also have a softer sound, just like the English **TS** that can be found in words like "cats":

Grazie (Thank You)

Ozio (Laziness)

Despite the rule that **Z** at the beginning of a word has a hard sound and the one inside the word has a soft sound, in reality, it changes a lot from individual to individual. Some people say *Zucchero* and *Zaino* both with a soft **Z** and vice versa, so there is no need to pay too much attention to this detail.

Double Consonants

In Italian, it is not so rare to find double letters. Actually, this happens almost all the time, to the point that if you wanted to translate this sentence that you are reading right now into Italian, you would find at least a dozen of them.

But how should you behave with this peculiarity of the Italian language?

Do not worry—it is not the case to be concerned about! A double letter simply indicates that the sound of the original consonant must be accentuated. Whether it has a soft or hard sound, it is enough to accentuate its presence by saying it for a slightly longer period than the usual pronunciation.

And with this, you have completed most of this language's peculiarities. As you can see, there are differences in pronunciation, but they are not so emphasized.

In addition, many consonants are missing from the list: so how do the rules work for them? They have not been added simply because they work in the same way as the English language.

Consonants such as **B, D, F, L, M,** and so on have the same English language pronunciation, which certainly makes it easy to learn the Italian pronunciation.

To sum up:

- **A** is pronounced as the **U** from the English word "**cut**".

- **E** is pronounced like the **E** from the English word "**rest**" or as the **E** of the English word "**appointment**".

- The **I** is pronounced like the **Y** from the English word "**baby**" or as the double **EE** from the word "**meet**".

- The **O** is pronounced like the **O** of the English word "**dog**".

- **U** is pronounced as the **U** from the English word "**loud**" or as the double **OO** of the word "**doom**".

- The **C** and the **G** can have a soft or hard sound. The soft sound is like the English words "**chilly**" and "**June**", while the hard sound is similar to the English words "**cat**" and "**gift**".

- If **GL** is followed by **I** or **E** (apart from rare exceptions), the sound will be soft and similar to the English word "**million**".

- **G** makes another sound thanks to the combinations of **N**. In this case, it will create a sound very similar to the Spanish letter **ñ.**

- **Q** is always pronounced as **K**, with a very hard sound.

- **SC** follows the same rules as **C**. In front of an **I** or **E** it has a soft sound like "**shoe**"; otherwise, it has a hard sound like for "**task**".

- The **S** can also have a hard or soft sound, depending on the word in which it is found. The soft sound is similar to the **S** in the English word "**still**", while the hard sound comes close to **Z**, in words like "**zebra**".

- **Z** can have a harder sound (especially if found at the beginning of a sentence) or a softer sound (if found within the sentence instead); in the latter, it is similar to the English's **TS** sound ("**cats**").

• When you come across double consonants, such as **CC, LL, MM**, and so on, it simply means that the sound of the mentioned consonant must be emphasized. You can do this by making it sound slightly longer than usual.

As mentioned at the beginning of the section, pronunciation is a delicate subject to be improved, and it takes a long time before reaching a level where you won't be recognized as an outsider while speaking the Italian language.

This brief guide will help you to deal with Italian words more confidently and invite you to read the words in the next pages aloud, by yourself, while trying to follow the advice given in this chapter.

In what other ways can you improve your Italian pronunciation? You can follow a rule applied to every language: try to sing the Italian songs you like, watch Italian movies in the original language, and try to pronounce as much as possible those words you may find difficult.

The most complicated step that you will have to face regarding Italian pronunciation is the soft sounds. For this reason, this aspect is highlighted several times, mostly because in other languages (like English) hard sounds are more common.

Especially for certain consonants, it is natural to associate a hard sound to letters like **G** and **C**, when very often they actually have an altered soft sound.

Thus, please pay attention to this aspect so that you won't find any problems with these letters.

And remember: the way to correct pronunciation is a long but enjoyable path because it is full of small yet motivational goals.

Dictionary

It is not possible to write an entire Italian dictionary that fits into this book. However, the purpose of this manual is not to provide a too detailed understanding of the Italian language, but rather, to be a handbook for learning how to speak Italian quickly.

Thus, a chapter is dedicated to the words that are used more in the given examples and that you will often use in your sentences—to learn them quickly.

The words have been divided according to the context, and, for this reason, the chapter is not made so that you have to learn all the words listed below in a single session. This is a reference at your disposal so that at any time while reading this book or practicing a conversation, you can return to these pages and find the word you are looking for.

Family / Famiglia

Cognato/a	–	Brother/Sister-in-law
Famiglia	–	Family
Figlio/a	–	Son/Daughter
Fratello	–	Brother
Genero/a	–	Son/Daughter-in-law

Madre	–	Mother
Nonno/a	–	Grandfather/Grandmother
Padre	–	Father
Sorella	–	Sister
Suocero/a	–	Father/Mother-in-law
Zio/a	–	Uncle/Aunt
Nipote	–	Nephew/Niece
Parente–		Relative

Note: With this last word, it is usually called a "false friend". What is it all about?

This is a word that's very similar to another in Italian but has a different meaning. In this case, the situation becomes more complicated since both of these words fall within the family context.

The word "Parente" in Italian looks much "Parent" in English, but the meaning is different:

Parente–		Relative
Genitore	–	Parent

Having made this necessary clarification, here are the words concerning the family sphere:

Marito	–	Husband
Moglie	–	Wife
Cugino	–	Cousin

School / Scuola

Asilo	–	Kindergarten
Classe	–	Class
Compagno	–	Classmate

Compito in classe	–	Class assignment
Compito a casa	–	Homework
Penna	–	Pen
Matita	–	Pencil
Maestro	–	Teacher (primary school)
Quaderno	–	Exercise book
Professore	–	Professor
Zaino	–	Backpack
Ricreazione	–	Recess
Scuola Elementare	–	Primary school
Scuola Media	–	Middle school
Scuola Superiore	–	High school
Libro	–	Book
Calcolatrice	–	Calculator
Orologio	–	Clock
Gomma	–	Eraser

This last word is particular, as its direct translation is "Rubber". In fact, the word "Gum" indicates both the instrument used to delete and the material itself.

Colla	–	Glue
Mappa	–	Map
Righello	–	Ruler
Forbici	–	Scissors

Work / Lavoro

Assunto	–	Hired

Collega	–	Colleague
Computer	–	Computer
Licenziato	–	Fired
Orario di lavoro	–	Working time
Pausa Pranzo	–	Lunch break
Scrivania	–	Desk
Stipendio	–	Salary
Straordinari	–	Overtime
Turno	–	Work shift

Food / Cibo – Beverage / Bevande

Acqua	–	Water
Acqua frizzante	–	Sparkling water
Ananas	–	Pineapple
Aglio	–	Onion
Basilico	–	Basil
Birra	–	Beer
Carne	–	Meat
Formaggio	–	Cheese
Lasagna	–	Lasagna
Latte	–	Milk
Melanzana	–	Eggplant
Pane	–	Bread
Pasta	–	Pasta
Peperone	–	Pepper (peperone, not pepperoni)
Pesce	–	Fish

Pizza	–	Pizza
Prosciutto	–	Ham
Salame	–	Salami
Spaghetti	–	Spaghetti
Succo di frutta	–	Fruit juice
Tonno	–	Tuna
Uovo	–	Egg
Vino	–	Wine

[Note: Coca Cola and Fanta are called as their brand. Soda is a different drink in Italy]

Time and Weather – Tempo (same meaning)

Secondo	–	Second
Minuto	–	Minute
Ora	–	Hour
Giorno	–	Day
Settimana	–	Week
Mese	–	Month
Anno	–	Year
Sole	–	Sun
Pioggia	–	Rain
Nebbia	–	Fog
Nuvoloso	–	Cloudy
Neve	–	Snow

[Note: You will see the days of the week and months of the year in the dedicated section, as included in the manual is a slight in-depth analysis that you should find interesting.]

Prepositions

Di	–	Of
A	–	To
Da	–	From
In	–	In
Con	–	With
Su	–	Up
Per	–	Through
Tra	–	Between
Fra	–	Between

These prepositions are not useful words like the ones seen so far, but they are very present in the various Italian sentences, and, for this reason, are on this list.

Similar to these words, there are other terms usually used in the construction of sentences, such as:

Davanti	–	In front
Dietro	–	Behind
Dopo	–	After
Fuori	–	Out of
Lontano	–	Far
Mediante	–	With (just like "con")
Prima	–	Before
Sopra	–	On
Sotto	–	Under

Within this chapter, you saw what is called a "false friend"—a term that may seem to have one meaning, but instead, means something else.

Since these terms are insidious, the main false friends that are created between Italian and English will now be listed.

False Friends

Before reviewing the list below, this is how the table works. On the left of the table is the English term you are familiar with, and at its right, is the correct Italian translation of the term. On the right of the table is the Italian term similar to the English word but with a different meaning, which is reported on the far right.

To give an example:

"To annoy" is translated into Italian with "Infastidire", while the Italian verb "Annoiare" is translated into English with "To bore".

It seems clear that these two terms have a very different meaning, but despite this, many people confuse the two terms, even in professional translations that then reach the small and big screen.

It is not essential to know all of these words, but if you have any doubts, you can find the answers in this list.

English word	Translation in Italian	Italian False Friend	Meaning of the false friend
Convenience	Comodità	Convenienza	Profit
Corpse	Cadavere	Corpo	Body
Definitely	Certamente	Definitivamente	Ultimately
Delusion	Illusione	Delusione	Disappointment
Disgrace	Vergogna	Disgrazia	Misfortune
Disposable	Usa e getta	Disponibile	Available
Editor	Redattore	Editore	Publisher
Actual	Effettivo	Attuale	Present
Actually	In realtà	Attualmente	Currently
Addiction	Dipendenza	Addizione	Sum
To annoy	Infastidire	Annotare	To bore
To attack	Assalire	Attaccare	Stick
Educated	Colto	Educato	Polite
Education	Istruzione	Educazione	Upbringing
Entitled	Avente diritto a	Intitolato	Titled
Estate	Proprietà	Estate	Summer
Eventually	Alla fine	Eventualmente	Possibly
Factory	Fabbrica	Fattoria	Farm
Familiar	Ben conosciuto	Familiare	Related to family
Flipper	Pinna	Flipper	Pinball machine
Front	Facciata	La fronte	Forehead
Furniture	Mobili	Fornitura	Supply
Gracious	Clemente	Grazioso	Pretty
Gymnasium	Palestra	Ginnasio	High school
Inhabited	Abitato	Inabitato	Uninhabited
Injury	Ferita, lesione	Ingiuria	Insult
Large	Grande	Largo	Wide
Lecture	Conferenza	Lettura	Reading
Library	Biblioteca	Libreria	Bookshop
To license	Dare una licenza	Licenziare	To fire
Lunatic	Pazzo	Lunatico	Moody
Cave	Caverna, grotta	Cava	Quarry
Code	Codice	Coda	Tail
Cold	Freddo	Caldo	Hot
Commodity	Merce, prodotto	Comodità	Comfort
To con	Imbrogliare	Con	With
Luxury	Lusso	Lussuria	Lust
Magazine	Rivista	Magazzino	Warehouse
To magnify	Ingrandire	Magnificare	To praise

Mansion	Villa	*Mansione*	Duty
Mess	Confusione	*Messa*	Mass
Misery	Sofferenza	*Miseria*	Poverty
To attend	Assistere	*Attendere*	To wait
Attitude	Atteggiamento	*Attitudine*	Aptitude
Audience	Pubblico	*Udienza*	Hearing
To avert	Allontanare	*Avvertire*	To warn
Barracks	Caserma	*Baracca*	Shack, hut
Morbid	Morboso	*Morbido*	Soft, tender
To nominate	Proporre per una candidatura	*Nominare*	To name
Basket	Cesto	*Basket*	Basketball
Box	Scatola	*Box*	Garage
Brave	Coraggioso	*Bravo*	Good, clever
Camera	Macchina fotografica	*Camera*	Room
Camping	Il campeggiare	*Camping*	Campsite
Notice	Avviso	*Notizia*	News
Novel	Romanzo	*Novella*	Short story
To occur	Accadere	*Occorrere*	To need
Ostrich	Struzzo	*Ostrica*	Oyster
Parent	Genitore	*Parente*	Relative
Patent	Brevetto	*Patente*	Driver's license
Pavement	Marciapiede	*Pavimento*	Floor
Petrol	Benzina	*Petrolio*	Oil, petroleum
Prepared	Disposto a	*Preparato*	Trained
Preservative	Conservante	*Preservativo*	Condom
Presumption	Supposizione	*Presunzione*	Conceit
To pretend	Fingere, simulare	*Pretendere*	To claim, assume
To process	Elaborare	*Processare*	To put on trial
Proper	Appropriato	*Proprio*	One's own
Puzzle	Problema, enigma	*Puzzle*	Jigsaw puzzle
Rape	Stupro	*Rapa*	Turnip
Rate	Velocità, tasso	*Rate*	Instalments
To realize	Rendersi conto	*Realizzare*	Fulfil, carry out
Record	Disco	*Ricordo*	Memory
Concurrence	Coincidenza	*Concorrenza*	Competition
Confidence	Fiducia	*Confidenza*	Intimacy
Conservatory	Serra	*Conservatorio (di musica)*	School of music
Consistent	Coerente	*Consistente*	Substantial, large
To control	Dominare	*Controllare*	To check
Relevant	Pertinente	*Rilevante*	Remarkable

To retain	Conservare	*Ritenere*	To think, to believe
To retire	Andare in pensione	*Ritirare*	To withdraw
Romance	Storia d'amore	*Romanzo*	Novel
Rotten	Marcio	*Rotto*	Broken
Rumor	Pettegolezzo, diceria	*Rumore*	Noise
Sane	Equilibrato	*Sano*	Healthy
Scholar	Studioso	*Scolaro*	Pupil
Sensible	Sensato	*Sensibile*	Sensitive
Slip	Sottoveste	*Slip*	Briefs, knickers
Spot	Foruncolo, puntino	*Spot*	Advert, commercial
Candid	Schietto, sincero	*Candido*	Snow white
Canteen	Mensa, borraccia	*Cantina*	Cellar, wine shop
Case	Scatoletta	*Case*	Houses
Casual	Informale	*Casuale*	Chance
Caution	Cautela	*Cauzione*	Guarantee
Stamp	Francobollo	*Stampa*	Press
Suggestive	Allusivo	*Suggestivo*	Evocative
Sympathetic	Compassionevole	*Simpatico*	Likeable
Taste	Sapore	*Tasto*	Key, button
Toast	Pane tostato	*Brindisi, toast*	Toasted sandwich
Vacancy	Vuoto, posto vacante	*Vacanza*	Holiday, vacation
Verse	Strofa	*Verso*	Line

The Rule of the 5 W

As in the English language, in Italian, there are five interrogative particles, which are good to recognize in a sentence. The name "Rule of 5 W" arose from a journalistic guideline to answer the reader's questions, but the same principle will be explained here regarding how these particles work and translate into Italian.

So, let's start in alphabetical order.

What?

The literal translation of "What" is "Cosa", which is the most generic word that exists in the Italian language. Since "Cosa" can also be translated with "Thing", it is clear that it is widely used within the language.

This interrogative particle is used to gain information on a thing, plant or animal, but not a person.

Let's try to see it in a certain context and within an interrogative sentence:

"Cosa vuoi per cena?"

"What do you want for dinner?"

The purpose of this word is very similar to the English "What" and is also used to ask for clarifications if something is not clear.

Example:

P: "I hate you!" – "Io ti odio!"

A: "**What**?!" – "**Cosa**?!"

P: "You heard me!" – "Mi hai sentito!"

The only time when confusion might arise is when the "Cosa" is used as a translation of "Thing" since it is a double meaning.

So, even though the literal translation of "What" is "Cosa", sometimes it can also be translated as "Che".

Here is an example:

"What did you do yesterday?"

*"**Cosa** hai fatto ieri?"*

*"**Che** hai fatto ieri?"*

In both cases, the sentence has perfect sense. The "Che" is mainly used when you would ask information about a specific non-human thing. For example, when you would like to know what breed a dog is or a certain kind of plant:

"What breed is that dog?"

*"Di **che** razza è quel cane?"*

When?

"When" is used to identify a period of time, and in Italian, is translated as "Quando". This particle is then used in the sentences regarding a question or making a statement about a specific moment in time.

Here are some examples:

"When will we go to the sea?"

"Quando andremo al mare?"

In this case, luckily, there is no risk of confusing this word with another that has the same meaning (as in the "What" case).

Where?

"Where" is translated into "Dove" in Italian. This particle is found in sentences expressing a question or a statement about a specific place.

Here are some examples:

"Where do you live?"

"Dove abiti?"

"Where do we go to eat?"

"Dove andiamo a mangiare?"

Of course, just as in the previous cases, "Dove" can also be used in affirmative sentences:

"Here's where I live: in Rome."

"Ecco dove vivo: a Roma."

"That is the country where I was born."

"Quello è il Paese dove sono nato."

Unlike the word "What", this word has only one meaning, just as the word "When".

Who?

"Who" can be translated "Chi" in Italian. This particle is used to ask questions and information regarding a person.

A good example is:

"Who are you?"

"Chi sei tu?"

Why?

This is the most particular particle to remember. Unlike in English, where there are two words with the same meaning to be used in an interrogative or affirmative context (why and because), in Italian, you are faced with a single word: "Perché".

Here are some examples:

"Why did you call me?"

"Perché mi hai chiamato?"

"Because I need you."

"Perché ho bisogno di te."

As you can see, the same word is used in both Italian sentences.

Note: the last letter of the word "Perché" has an accent mark. This means, as explained in the chapter dedicated to pronunciation, that the final "e" must be pronounced strongly, like in the word "appointment".

Although it is possible to use the same word in both affirmative and negative sentences, some alternatives exist in Italian that can be used instead of that (but only in affirmative sentences).

Words like "Poiché" benefit from the same translation:

"I came because I needed you."

"Sono venuto poiché avevo bisogno di te."

Thus, ends your lesson on interrogative particles. As you can see, it is simply a matter of remembering what term the translation corresponds to. This way, you will immediately have an advantage in understanding a question and replying accordingly.

To sum up:

- "What" is translated into "Cosa" or "Che".
- "Where" is translated into "Dove".
- "When" is translated into "Quando".
- "Who" is translated into "Chi".
- "Why" is translated into "Perché" or "Poiché", but the latter only when the sentence is affirmative.

Ringraziare e Scusarsi (Being Thankful and Sorry)

As a fundamental part of many conversations (as you will see later in the section about asking directions), it is time to dedicate yourself to learning how to apologize or thank a person in Italian.

Although they may sound trivial, the words "thank you", "excuse me" and "I'm sorry" are part of everyday life.

You will start by studying this and learning, step by step, the language differences in Italian. For example, you will see how "excuse me" and "I'm sorry" are translated with the same word.

Let's start with "how to express gratitude" while learning one of the best-known Italian words right after "Ciao".

Grazie (Thank you)

This is a translation that will help you the most because "Thank you" is "Grazie" in Italian, a word perfect for any circumstance and whomever you are talking to.

As you will see in the coming chapters, the way of speaking, as well as the pronouns used, tend to change according to the situation (whether formal or informal). However, this doesn't occur with "Grazie".

As already stated, "Grazie" is really common in daily spoken Italian.

Sometimes, "Grazie" is combined with a pronoun, but only while responding to another person's gratitude. However, it is much easier to understand it with an example.

Here is a scenario to explain the concept:

Luca invites Marco to eat pasta at his house. Being grateful, Marco gives some eggs to Luca.

M: "Grazie per la pasta."

M: "Thank you for the pasta."

L: "**Grazie a te** per le uova."

L: "Thank you for the eggs."

As you can see, in the first sentence, "Grazie" is not combined by any pronoun and is followed by the reason for the gratitude.

In the second sentence, as a reply, Luca is being thankful to Marco for bringing him eggs.

Although "Grazie" can be used in every circumstance, there are specific cases in which you should express respect towards an important person, like a professor or employer.

Here, it is possible to use the word "La ringrazio" or "Grazie a Lei". "La ringrazio" can be used as gratitude opposed to "Grazie a te" (in this case "Lei" is used instead of "Te" since it is a rule in the formal Italian language).

Curiously, there is another formal, although extremely archaic, word of expressing gratitude: "Obbligato" (Obliged), which is very similar to the Portuguese word "Obrigado".

There are also other words to express gratitude. A more formal word, yet less used than others, is "Essere grato" (to be grateful), which is a verb that follows the conjugation of the verb Essere (a verb you will see later on).

Let's now move on and see how to apologize in Italian. You will also see in how many ways you can say "Scusa".

Scusa (Sorry)

One of the most complicated aspects of learning a language is when you have to face a word with multiple meanings, and "Scusa" is one of those. Let's analyze this word to help you use it correctly in a future conversation.

1) The most common translation is:

"Scusa" – "Sorry"

As in English, the Italian "Scusa" is used to apologize to others. However, unfortunately, if "Sorry" is translated into "Scusa", you cannot say the same for "I am sorry".

In this particular case, the most common translation is instead:

"Mi dispiace" – I'm sorry

What is the main difference? "Scusa" indicates an apology for something that was done/your fault; "Mi dispiace", however, can also be used when you have nothing to do with the problem you are facing.

Some examples are:

"Scusa per averti rotto la penna." – "Sorry for breaking your pen."

"Mi dispiace per la morte di tuo padre." – "I'm sorry for your father's death."

The difference is clear, but "Mi dispiace" can further be used for apologizing for what you have actually done:

"Mi dispiace per averti rotto la penna." – "Sorry for breaking your pen."

As you can see, the English translation has not changed at all; the difference lies in the original meaning of the word and not in its usual meaning. By saying "Scusa", you are asking forgiveness for the problem that occurred.

The complete sentence construction would actually be: "Scusami"—that means "Scusa me".

Saying "Mi dispiace" instead informs the other person that you are sorry for what happened to them.

These are just shades of the Italian language, but they are important to learn since it is always convenient to know when and how to apologize to others.

So, this is the real meaning of "Mi dispiace".

2) As mentioned before, "scusa" can have other meanings as well. It can be translated into "Excuse". In this particular case, it means a "Giustificazione" (justification), as in this example:

Marco: "Io sono stato malato; qual è la tua scusa?"

Marco: "I was sick; what's your excuse?"

To sum up:

- "Thank you" is translated into "Grazie", which can be used in every context and with any person. Despite this, to show respect to a person you do not know or toward an older person, you should use the word "La ringrazio" while using the pronoun "Lei".

- "I'm sorry" can be translated into "Mi dispiace". It is used to demonstrate sorrow for a certain event external to you. Saying "Scusa" instead asks for forgiveness for something you did.

- The word "Scusa" has many other translations, such as "Excuse".

The Construction of the Sentence

Despite the differences between English and Italian, the sentence structure is very similar.

Let's start by looking at a simple sentence:

John *eats* <u>a</u> **sandwich**

John *mangia* <u>un</u> **panino**

The number of words, in this case, is the same, and it is easy to understand which English word corresponds to the Italian one.

In learning Italian, the luck is that it uses the same alphabet as English. The two languages have also influenced each other in the past and continue to do so today.

There are Anglo-Saxon words that have been contaminated by the Latin: think of "Tooth" and "Dentist". The translation of "Dentist" in Italian is "Dentista"—very similar.

Despite this, it will be necessary to develop a vocabulary to understand the different sentences—however, one thing at a time. First, you need to understand how to construct a sentence and then learn all the words.

The biggest difference in the construction of the sentence that runs between the English and the Italian is the interrogative form. While in English, the subject and the verb change position in formulating a question, in Italian, this does not happen.

Here is the phrase:

Is she married? **She is** married.

In Italian, it becomes:

Lei è sposata? **Lei è** sposata.

As you can see, the subject remains in the same position even in the interrogative form.

This is an important aspect since you are looking at the same sentence's structure. And it is the base of all the Italian grammar, so naturally, you may experience difficulties in switching between English and Italian.

Always remember: Italian sentences follow a specific order:

Subject – Verb – Article – Object + Any other elements

Even if there may be differences in this regard, made by a simple personal taste (it is possible to move the elements within the sentence while maintaining their meaning, even at the disadvantage of the sentence's fluency), this rule applies to most Italian sentences.

Here are some examples:

Carl eats an apple – Carl mangia una mela

Carl – subject – *Carl*

Mangia – the singular third person of the verb to "Mangiare" (to eat) – *Eats*

Una – feminine article – *An*

Mela – object – *Apple*

As you can see, both sentences have the same structure and the same number of words (obviously, this is not always the case, but the differences are not as marked as you could imagine). Everything changes with any interrogative form. Even the most basic question:

Hi, John, how are you?

Becomes:

Ciao, John, come stai?

Let's analyze this sentence:

Ciao – greeting – *Hi*

John – proper noun – *John*

Come – adverb – *How*

Stai – The second-person singular of the verb to "Stare" (to stay) – Are

Many differences emerge from a single sentence. The first is that, in Italian, the verb "Stare" (to stay) is used instead of the verb "Essere" (to be). In this particular case, it is a person's health and indicates that person's condition.

The second big difference is that, in Italian, the pronoun "Tu" has disappeared, as it has been overlooked. However, you will focus more on this topic in another section.

Had it not been overlooked, the position of the word "Tu" would have been:

Ciao, John, tu come stai?

As you can see, while in English the pronoun "you" has been placed at the end of the sentence, in Italian, it remains at the beginning of the sentence.

It is a difficult difference to master, but it is important to remember it to speak fluent Italian.

The Neutral Gender

You can further see the big difference between English and Italian on the list of the various pronouns:

I	Io
You	Tu
He/She/It	Lui/Lei
We	Noi
You	Voi
They	Loro (or Essi)

As you can see, in Italian, the equivalent of the pronoun "it" is not present. In fact, the neutral gender does not exist, and every word is either male or female.

Even inanimate objects have a gender. Here are some examples:

The chair – La sedia (female)

The book – Il libro (male)

Unfortunately, there is no precise rule that establishes when the male form should be used or when you should opt for the female one. Only experience can help you in this sense.

The Other Genders

As you will see in the following chapters, the gender of a word plays a crucial role for the article used with it (read the dedicated chapter on articles). So how is it possible to understand the genre of a word at first sight?

As with other examples, experience still plays an important role, but it is possible thanks to a small trick to understanding it in 90 percent of cases.

Usually, if words are ending with the vowel A, they are feminine, while those ending with the vowel O are masculine. Of course, this is not true in all cases, but it is good to make an initial selection of words.

Then there are words ending with other vowels. How do they work? Usually, there are names ending in –E, and although part of them are masculine, this is not always true. Some examples are:

Il prete (male) – The priest

Il mese (male) – The month

La rete (female) – The web

La pelle (female) –The skin

So, as mentioned before, it is only experience that can save you from any potential error. It is also necessary to pay even more attention, as there are words that may appear to be of a certain gender but turn out to be another.

For example:

La moto (female) – The motorcycle

As you can see, the word ends with the vowel O but is still a feminine word. Why? Because, in this case, it is the short version. The complete word would be "Motocicletta", which is feminine and keeps the same gender even in the short version.

Of course, some words end with a consonant, but their number is low compared to others, and for this reason, it is enough to remember their specific gender. Also, many of these have foreign and/or Latin origins, such as:

Il gol – *Male*

Il bar – *Male*

Lo sport – *Male*

L'email – *Female*

Il gas – *Male*

Speaking of masculine and feminine gender, another aspect to take into consideration is that while there are words that belong to one gender, there are many others that can belong to both of them, such as:

Amico – *Friend (male)*

Amica – *Friend (female)*

As you can see, the words that refer to a person or animal, overall support both genders because a person or animal can show themselves belonging to a certain sexual gender.

Is it enough to change the letter O with an A, then? Usually, yes, but let's see some examples:

Maestro – *Teacher (male)*

Maestra – *Teacher (female)*

Ladro – *Thief (male)*

Ladra – *Thief (female)*

Poliziotto – *Police officer (male)*

Poliziotta – *Police officer (female)*

But it is not always like this because not every word ends with the letter O or A. Let's think about, for instance, words that refer to people but end with an E:

Dottore – *Medic (male)*

Dottoressa – *Medic (female)*

Leone – *Lion*

Leonessa – *Lioness*

Principe – *Prince*

Principessa – *Princess*

As you can see from the examples above, in most of these cases, there is a change from -E to -ESSA. This rule has its exceptions, though, as there are names that end in –O, but in feminine words still become -ESSA:

Soldato – *Soldier (male)*

Soldatessa – Soldier (female)

In addition, there is a whole series of irregular names that have a real and separated form from these rules, such as:

Attore – *Actor*

Attrice – *Actress*

It is hard to remember all of these differences, except with experience, but usually, the names work as seen above.

Note: although the names that often end with E are considered masculine, it is good to remember that most of the feminine singular names that end with A, obtain an E in their plural.

Let's look at some examples:

Donna (woman)	Donne (women)
Borsa (bag)	Borse (bags)
Gatta (female cat)	Gatte (cats)

It is quite simple to distinguish one word from the singular masculine and one from the feminine in the plural. So, with a little attention, you should have no problem.

However, this aspect was worth underlining to avoid any potential mistake made in good faith.

The Pronoun "You"

Another fundamental difference that runs between English and Italian is the translation of the pronoun "You".

While in English, "You" can refer both to one or more people, in Italian, there are two distinct words. "Tu" is the singular pronoun and "Voi" is the plural form.

Let's look at some examples:

You are John

Tu sei John

You are John and Michael

Voi siete John e Michael

This difference is easy to master because it is sufficient to remember which pronoun should be used in front of one or more people.

The Pronoun "Lei"

In the list of the pronouns seen above, "Lei" is the literal translation of "She". Unfortunately, this is not always the case, as "lei" also assumes a different meaning based on the context.

In English, whether you are addressing a friend or an employer, the pronoun "You" is always used. In Italian, the situation is quite different.

While the translation "Tu" can be used in informal environments, when you talk to people you don't know or who have a position above yours (teachers, employers, seniors), you must use the pronoun "Lei" instead of "Tu".

Since this concept is a bit complicated, here are some examples:

Talking to a friend: "**Tu** sei John?" (Are you John?)

Talking to a stranger: "**Lei** è John?" (Are you John?)

Even if the meaning of the sentence in English has not changed, another pronoun is used in Italian. The literal English translation of the second sentence would be "Is she John?", which, of course, makes no sense.

Although this is a difficult aspect to master, it is also very important because it's the best way to convey courtesy in a formal environment.

Sometimes people use the pronoun "Voi" (plural You) or "Loro" (They) instead of "Lei" in communicating in an extremely formal way. Don't worry though: this is an archaic construction, and it is only used in specific regions of Southern Italy.

This, however, should not make you think that this aspect is not important: giving the "Tu" to a person you are not familiar with can be offensive and bad manners—based on the person you are talking to.

As you will soon see, most of the Italian personal pronouns can be left out from the sentences without changing their meanings.

Just in case you address a person with "Lei", this pronoun is almost always highlighted and not left out, to maintain the formalities between two people interacting with each other.

The Implied Pronoun

So far, you have seen three major differences, but unfortunately, the differences in the use of pronouns do not end here.

Let's now talk about the implicit pronouns.

While in English the pronoun or subject of a sentence is always specified, in Italian, it is often eliminated from the sentence as it is not necessary.

Example:

I am hungry.

(**Io**) ho fame.

You can see the pronoun in the Italian sentence between parenthesis because it is often omitted in the spoken language. In fact, the sentence without a pronoun, "Ho fame", makes perfect sense as it is.

Don't worry though: using the pronoun within the sentence is not wrong. You can also translate it with "Io ho fame", and the sentence will be correct anyway.

With time and experience, you will learn when it is possible to cut the pronoun from the sentence without losing its meaning.

This difference is mentioned just so that you are not confused when the pronoun is not specified in a sentence.

Of course, any pronoun you saw earlier can be left out from an Italian sentence. Actually, it is more common not saying the initial pronoun since it could sound too forced in the sentences.

Let's see some examples of sentences used in everyday life where the pronouns have been omitted:

- *Mi passi il sale?* – Can you pass me the salt?

This is a very common sentence, and, as you can see, it does not contain any first pronouns. It is also an interrogative form, so it is worth analyzing it to show once again the differences between Italian and English.

(Tu) – Second singular person, pronoun removed – *You*

Mi – First singular person (you will better see this pronoun in the next section) – *Me*

Passi – Second singular person verb to "Passare" (to pass) – *Pass*

Il – Male article– *The*

Sale – *Salt*

Once again, you can see that while in English the subject comes after the verb, in Italian, it is found (if not omitted) at the beginning of the sentence.

The second singular person "Tu" is almost always left out, like "Io" because it is easy to understand that if you are talking about yourself or talking straight to your interlocutor, it is not necessary to repeat the pronoun. The same can be said for "Noi" and "Voi", the plural version of the first and second person, even if the omission is much less marked in this case.

Curiously, the pronoun can be said in two particular cases:

- When an alternative is proposed to a previous statement.

To see this, imagine a chat between Marco and Luca, who are discussing where to go with their friend for the holidays:

Marco: "(Noi) Vorremmo andare in montagna, quest'anno…"

Marco: "We would like to go to the mountains this year…"

Luca: "Noi vogliamo andare al mare."

Luca: "We want to go to the sea."

As you can see, in Marco's sentences, the "Noi" (We) pronoun is not specified, while in Luca's response, he is using the pronoun to highlight that his group has a different will.

Here's another example:

Antonio: "Ho già mangiato oggi."

Antonio: "I already ate today."

Andrea: "Io ho ancora fame."

Andrea: "I'm still hungry."

This example follows the rule stated before as well.

- When the rest of the sentence is implied.

In this case, the pronoun becomes essential as the whole sentence is left out. Often this form is connected to the previous one, as it can be shown as a response to a previous statement.

Here's an example:

Marco: "Andiamo in montagna?"

Marco: "Let's go to the mountains?"

Luca: "Io no."

Luca: "Not me."

In this case, the personal pronoun has been specified because if Luca would have replied with only "No," it could have mean blocking the whole group rather than expressing a personal choice.

These are, however, extremely particular cases, so it is generally possible to identify the implied pronoun by checking the verb within the sentence. Since each person has their own conjugation of the verb (as you will see in the chapter dedicated to this element of the sentence), it is easy to identify the subject of a sentence even if it is not specified.

The Object Pronoun

What has been analyzed so far has only been the personal pronoun as a subject. Another great aspect to take into consideration, regarding sentence construction, is the personal pronoun as an object.

You know the English equivalent, but how does the Italian behave in this sense?

Me	Me/Mi
You	Te/Ti
Him	Lo/Gli
Her	La/Le
Us	Noi/Ci
You	Voi/Vi
Them	Loro/li

The neutral is not reported because it does not exist in Italian—it simply follows the rules of Him/Her.

As you can see from this brief outline, all personal pronouns as objects have a double form in Italian.

This is because the sentence can always be formulated in two different ways and, in particular, there is what is commonly called "integration of the pronoun". This means that sometimes the pronoun can be integrated into the verb.

Don't worry: here are some examples to help you understand:

I know **him**.

(Io) **lo** conosco.

This is the basic case. As you can see, the subject is again in brackets because it can be eliminated and the object pronoun "him" becomes "lo".

I talk to **him**.

Gli parlo io.

In this case, the object pronoun is still "him", but in Italian, it becomes "Gli" due to the construction "to him".

I sent **him** a letter

Gli ho mandato una lettera

In this case, the pronoun "Gli" is used because the sentence can also be formulated as "I sent a letter to him".

Understanding how this type of pronoun works is simpler than one would think, as everyone behaves the same way.

Note: the use of Lo/Gli and La/Le is often mistaken by native Italians, just as "Your" and "You're" is often mistaken by native English speakers.

Let's look at a more complicated case:

Could you bring **me** a glass of water?

Mi puoi portare un bicchiere d'acqua?

As mentioned earlier, the object pronoun can be integrated within the same verb. Thus, the initial "Mi" of the sentence moves to the end of the verb:

Puoi portar**mi** un bicchiere d'acqua?

However, even in this case, it is a nuance of the more advanced language that you can get with experience. For the moment, just keep in mind the different pronoun objects that can be used in Italian.

The Adjective and the Possessive Pronoun

Although there are many different types of pronouns, the purpose of this book is to be as direct and simple as possible. For this reason, this section talks about another aspect of fundamental importance in the construction of sentences: possessive adjectives, which are different according to the subject in question:

My	Mio/a
Your	Tuo/a
His	Suo
Her	Sua
Its	Suo/a
Our	Nostro/a
Your	Vostro/a
Their	Loro

There are many things to say about these adjectives, so let's go in order.

Starting from the first, you immediately notice that the equivalents of "My", "Our" and "Your" have a double form. "My" can become "Mio" or "Mia" based on the gender of the object in question.

As mentioned earlier, every word in Italian is either male or female, and the gender of the word also influences the personal adjective.

Here's a direct example:

That is **my** house.

Quella è la **mia** casa.

In this case, the adjective "mia" is used because "casa" is a female word. If it were a male word, it would have been:

He is **my** brother.

Lui è **mio** fratello.

Of course, when talking about inanimate objects, it could be more difficult to understand this difference, as it is necessary to adapt the neutral English to the Italian gender. In fact, the direct translation of "His" and "Her" is simply "Suo" and "Sua".

Remember also that "Your", in Italian, changes based on whether the subject is a single person or more people. In the first case, it will be "Tuo", and in the second, it will be "Vostro".

Imagine a waiter showing customers to a table:

(One person)

This is **your** table.

Questo è il **tuo** tavolo.

(Two people)

This is **your** table.

Questo è il **vostro** tavolo.

Fortunately, the situation is not complicated by talking about possessive pronouns, as they are generally equal to adjectives:

Mine	Mio/a
Yours	Tuo/a

His	Suo
Hers	Sua
Ours	Nostro/a
Yours	Vostro/a
Theirs	Loro

As you can see, nothing changes, but be careful: the article generally anticipates the possessive pronoun.

Example:

This bag is **mine.**

Questa borsa è *la* **mia.**

To sum up:

- In Italian, there is no neutral gender; every word is female or male.

- The pronoun "You" is translated as "Tu" when referred to a single person and as "Voi" when referred to more than one person.

- In formal environments, "You" behaves as if it were the pronoun "She".

- Very often the pronoun is implied in Italian sentences.

- In Italian, the object pronoun can be integrated into verbs.

- In Italian, the possessive adjective and the possessive pronoun are equal, but the second is preceded by an article.

- In Italian, usually, the names ending with -O are masculine while the ones ending with -A are feminine. Names ending with -E belong to both categories.

- Some names can be both masculine and feminine, depending on the person or animal's gender that they belong to. In this case, usually, the masculine name ending with -O will end with an -A if feminine and masculine names ending with -E will end with -ESSA if feminine.

This is probably one of the more difficult chapters of the book, but it is also one of the most important, and, no matter how heavy it is to deal with, it is essential to understand the most common phrases in Italian.

How Verbs Are Conjugated

The second essential part for understanding an Italian sentence is the verb. In this sense, there is good news and bad news. The good news is that most verbs are conjugated in the same way, so if you manage to learn one, you will understand them all.

Unfortunately, though, many irregular verbs have their own behavior, but this will be discussed later.

Let's start with the two fundamental verbs in each language: "to be" and "to have".

"To be", present:

I am	Io sono
You are	Tu sei
He is	Lui è
She is	Lei è
We are	Noi siamo
You are	Voi siete
They are	Loro sono

"To have", present:

I have	Io ho

You have	Tu hai
He has	Lui ha
She has	Lei ha
We have	Noi abbiamo
You have	Voi avete
They have	Loro hanno

As you can see, while in English, the form of the verb changes just twice in all conjugations, every person in Italian has a different verbal form.

There is no other way to learn these verbs except by using your memory. For this reason, you will have to arm yourself with patience and dedicate some time to this section.

-are, -ere & -ire

Before analyzing the various verbal forms in the Italian language, it is good to take a step back and identify verb types that can be encountered. Basically, the infinitive forms of Italian verbs can end in three different ways: -are, -ere or -ire.

Here are some examples taken from the most used verbs in Italian:

-ARE:

Mangiare (*to eat*)

Camminare (*to walk*)

Studiare (*to study*)

Lavorare (*to work*)

Parlare (*to talk*)

-ERE:

Bere (*to drink*)

Sedere (*to sit*)

Scegliere (*to choose*)

Cadere (*to fall*)

Chiedere (*to ask*)

-IRE:

Dire (*to say*)

Capire (*to understand*)

Partire (*to leave*)

Why is it so important to highlight this aspect? Because depending on the infinitive's type, you will find a different conjugation of the various persons.

For this reason, in the next paragraphs, a practical example of each one of these terminations is offered, for each verbal time that will be analyzed, to better understand the difference between the various verb forms.

The Present

Except for irregular verbs, most verbal forms behave the same way.

Take, for example, the present of the verb "Mangiare" (to eat):

I eat	Io mang**io**
You eat	Tu mang**i**
He eats	Lui mang**ia**
She eats	Lei mang**ia**
We eat	Noi mang**iamo**
You eat	Voi mang**iate**
They eat	Loro mang**iano**

As seen above, the last letters of each verb were highlighted because it is how a verb is conjugated. The root "mangi" is the same as the infinitive "**mangi**are". At this point, the same letters are always added.

Let's take another verb and see how it behaves. This is the case, for example, for the verb "Camminare" (to walk):

I walk   Io cammin**o** (cammin + o)

You walk   Tu cammin**i** (cammin + i)

He walks   Lui cammin**a** (cammin + a)

She walks   Lei cammin**a** (cammin + a)

We walk   Noi cammin**iamo** (cammin + iamo)

You walk   Voi cammin**ate** (cammin + ate)

They walk   Loro cammin**ano** (cammin + ano)

By learning how the verb conjugates for different pronouns, you can use almost all the verbs. That said, sometimes there may be small differences in the vowels.

Here's another example, the verb "Dormire" (to sleep):

I sleep   Io dorm**o**

You sleep   Tu dorm**i**

He sleeps   Lui dorm**e** (dorm + e)

She sleeps   Lei dorm**e** (dorm + e)

We sleep   Noi dormi**amo**

You sleep   Voi dorm**ite** (dorm + ite)

They sleep   Loro dorm**ono**

Let's see the most common verbs that follow the traditional conjugation:

Mangiare (to eat)

Presentare (to introduce)

Imparare (to learn)

Lavorare (to work)

Studiare (to study)

Vivere (to live)

Dormire (to sleep)

Pagare (to pay)

How do you conjugate verbs? Simple: first, you need to identify the root. To do this, it is usually sufficient to remove the final part -are / -ere / -ire to the verb at the infinitive:

Mangi-are

Present-are

Impar-are

Lavor-are

Dorm-ire

Sed-ere (to sit)

At this point, add the final letters seen earlier. Let's say you want to use the phrase "He eats":

Take the root of "to eat": mangi-

Add the vowel relative to the third-person singular: -a

And here is the sentence: "Lui mangia".

Once this is established, you are going to complete the section dedicated to the present with the third conjugation, -ERE, of which you have not seen an example in this part yet.

To do this, you will use the verb "Bere: (to drink):

Io bev**o**   I drink

Tu bev**i**   You drink

Lui beve	He drinks
Lei beve	She drinks
Noi beviamo	We drink
Voi bevete	You drink
Loro bevono	They drink

As you can see, there are not many differences between the verbs that end with -IRE, -ERE or –ARE—if not with some vowels within the various conjugations.

Irregular Verbs

The rules you have seen before are valid in most cases, and in this next section, you will use the regular verbal forms for the examples.

Keep in mind that there are the irregular verbs. One of the most used verbs is "Andare" (to go), which behaves quite uniquely in the conjugation:

I go	Io vado
You go	Tu vai
He goes	Lui va
She goes	Lei va
We go	Noi andiamo
You go	Voi andate
They go	Loro vanno

As you can see, the verb turns out to be irregular because its root changes during the conjugation. Only the first and the second plural person keeps the same root as the infinitive.

From this point of view, even the verbs "Essere" and "Avere" can be considered irregular because their root changes during their conjugation, but since they are the main verbs of each language, it is normal that they have their own separate rule.

The Past

You will study all the tenses: most of them are essential for normal communication and are related to an advanced study of Italian.

The two tenses that you will be dealing with in this manual are the past and the future, as they are the most used in common Italian.

Speaking of the past, there are two forms: the past "Imperfetto", which indicates a continuous action in the past, and the "Remoto" past, which indicates a finished action far in the past.

A third form of the past is the "Passato Prossimo", and that is what you will see now because it is the most used and easiest to learn.

Present Perfect

Let's look at the verb "Mangiare" (to eat) as an example:

I ate	Io ho mangiato
You ate	Tu hai mangiato
He/She ate	Lui/Lei ha mangiato
We ate	Noi abbiamo mangiato
You ate	Voi avete mangiato
They ate	Loro hanno mangiato

How does the construction of this tense work? Simply take the present of the verb "to have" or "to be" (every verb requires one in particular) and add the past participle of the verb itself:

Io (first-person singular)

ho (first-person singular of the verb "to have")

mangiato (past participle)

Getting the past participle is very simple: just take the root mentioned before (mangia-) and add -**to**.

Here are some examples:

Dormire (to sleep) – **Dormi**to

Camminare (to walk) – **Cammina**to

Studiare (to study) – **Studia**to

In this regard, it is good to remember that there are verbs that work in a particular way in this case as well. As, for example, the verb "Leggere" (to read): the present perfect of this verb is "Letto", a verbal form in which it loses the consonant GG.

Which present should be used between "to be" and "to have"?

"To have" is used with:

- Transitive verbs: I read a book – Io **ho** letto un libro

- Verbs of movement, like walking.

 On the other hand, "to be" is used with transitive verbs.

After having seen a conjugation's example of -ARE, this time, you will see an example of the conjugation in –ERE. Since you already saw above that the present perfect of the verb to read is "Leggere", let's use just this verbal form:

Io ho letto	I read
Tu hai letto	You read
Lui ha letto	He read
Lei ha letto	She read
Noi abbiamo letto	We read
Voi avete letto	You read
Loro hanno letto	They read

As you can see, the present perfect is one of the easiest verbal forms to learn after learning the present, as it always uses the present of "avere" or "essere", followed by the participle.

For the conjugation -IRE and the last example, you are going to use a verb that requires the verb "essere" in its construction, "Partire":

Io sono partito	I left
Tu sei partito	You left
Lui è partito	He left
Lei è partita	She left
Noi siamo partiti	We left
Voi siete partiti	You left
Loro sono partiti	They left

Things get a little more complicated when it comes to talking about the Imperfect.

Imperfect

The imperfect is a verbal form that expresses a continuous action in the past. While the present perfect identifies something recently accomplished, the imperfect is the ideal if you want to indicate extended action for a certain period in the past.

How is this verbal form created? In most cases, it is enough to take the present and add -AV (if -ARE), -EV (if -ERE) or -IV (if -IRE) between the root and its conclusion.

A practical example is with the verb "Mangiare" (to eat). In the present:

Io mangio	I eat
Tu mangi	You eat
Lui mangia	He eats
Lei mangia	She eats
Noi mangiamo	We eat
Voi mangiate	You eat

Loro <u>mangi</u>**ano**	They eat

In the example seen above, the root of the verb is underlined, and its final part is in bold. Let's now see how the imperfect is formulated. To do this, italics have highlighted the added part:

Io <u>mangi</u>*av*o	I ate
Tu <u>mangi</u>*av*i	You ate
Lui <u>mangi</u>*av*a	He ate
Lei <u>mangi</u>*av*a	She ate
Noi <u>mangi</u>*av*amo	We ate
Voi <u>mangi</u>*av*ate	You ate
Loro <u>mangi</u>*av*ano	They ate

As you can see, it is quite simple to express the imperfect once you understand the present. As usual, let's look at an example with the conjugation with –ERE. In this case, "Read" (t*o read*):

Io leggevo	I read
Tu leggevi	You read
Lui leggeva	He read
Lei leggeva	She read
Noi leggevamo	We read
Voi leggevate	You read
Loro leggevano	They read

So, therefore, let's see an example of the third conjugation, the one ending with -IRE. In this case, "Capire" (to understand):

Io capivo	I understood
Tu capivi	You understood
Lui capiva	He understood

Lei capiva	She understood
Noi capivamo	We understood
Voi capivate	You understood
Loro capivano	They understood

While the rule of the "present" + av/iv/ev is often used, it is not always correct. For example, the present of "capire" (to understand) is:

Io capisco	I understand

While the past is:

Io capivo	I understood

As you can see, the word has changed from the present to the past, losing the consonants "sc".

Always remember: the imperfect states an ongoing action that happened in the past.

Let's now see the last type of past that you will study in this guide: the Simple Past.

Simple Past

The Simple Past can easily be considered the opposite of the Imperfect. While, as you have seen before, the Imperfect indicates an ongoing action in the past, the Simple Past indicates an accomplished action that took place a long time ago.

So, you cannot use it to talk about the movie you saw last week or even three months ago: the Simple Past period concerns years and its use is less highlighted compared to the ones you have learned so far, but nonetheless, is as important as them.

The Simple Past turns out to be more complicated than the two alternatives that came first, so take all the time you need to understand it.

In fact, this verbal form has its own conjugation, which cannot be traced back to the addition of letters as in the previous cases. Let's look at it using the first conjugation in -ARE, always with the verb "to eat" (*to eat*):

Io mangi**ai**	I ate
Tu mangi**asti**	You ate
Lui mangi**ò**	He ate
Lei mangi**ò**	She ate
Noi mangi**ammo**	We ate
Voi mangi**aste**	You ate
Loro mangi**arono**	They ate

As you can see, the Simple Past presents itself in a completely original form compared to the other verbal forms, and for this reason, it must be remembered.

For the sake of completeness, let's once again see the other two conjugations, with the verb "Leggere" (*to read)* and the verb "Dormire" (*to sleep):*

Io lessi	I read
Tu leggesti	You read
Lui lesse	He read
Lei lesse	She read
Noi leggemmo	We read
Voi leggeste	You read
Loro lessero	They read

As you can see in this case, the word's root changes, losing the two GG, just as it happened with the participle, which in this case is replaced by two SS.

Io dormii	I slept

Tu dormisti	You slept
Lui dormì	He slept
Lei dormì	She slept
Noi dormimmo	We slept
Voi dormiste	You slept
Essi dormirono	They slept

Unfortunately, there are not many other tips as it is, in reality, a more mnemonic exercise. Remember, however, that by knowing the Present Perfect and the Imperfect, you will still find yourself with an excellent ability to describe the past.

So, take your time and study the Simple Past with all the patience you need.

Of course, there are many other articulate verbal forms to describe the past, but as previously mentioned, these lessons provide something different than a usual grammar book.

In this guide, lessons are given on the sentence's construction and the elements that compose it, in order to help you better understand most of the common Italian sentences.

Now it is time to see what the future holds for you because, in the next section, you are going to learn about the future dedicated verbs.

The Future

The future is another commonly used verbal form and is the first that uses the much-known Italian accents. Let's see a classical conjugation of this verb:

I will eat	Io mangerò
You will eat	Tu mangerai
He will eat	Lui mangerà
She will eat	Lei mangerà

We will eat	Noi mang**eremo**
You will eat	Voi mang**erete**
They will eat	Loro mang**eranno**

Although it may seem complicated to look at, it is simpler than one might think because, once you learn the terminations of the various conjugations, they will be the same for almost all verbs:

I will study	Io studi**erò**
You will study	Tu studi**erai**
He/She will study	Lui/Lei studi**erà**
We will study	Noi studi**eremo**
You will study	Voi studi**erete**
They will study	Loro studi**eranno**

Let's see how the conjugation's verb with -ERE works while using the verb "Cadere" (*to fall*):

Io cadrò	I will fall
Tu cadrai	You will fall
Lui cadrà	He will fall
Lei cadrà	She will fall
Noi cadremo	We will fall
Voi cadrete	You will fall
Loro cadranno	They will fall

As you can see, the verb works in the same way even in this particular case. So, let's see the third conjugation with -IRE using the verb "Pulire" (*to clean*):

Io pulirò	I will clean
Tu pulirai	You will clean

Lui pulirà	He will clean
Lei pulirà	She will clean
Noi puliremo	We will clean
Voi pulirete	You will clean
Loro puliranno	They will clean

Even if the Italian forms are much more complicated than the English ones, as they change shape with each person, once you understand these verbal forms, you can communicate naturally with a native speaker.

Despite you having dealt with two heavy topics one after the other, the personal pronouns and the verbs, it was essential to talk about these two elements of the sentence right away so that they could be used in common phrases in the following chapters.

Don't worry: just one final step and you will be able to move on to a much lighter topic—talking about articles and numbers in Italian culture and language.

To sum up:

- The majority of Italian verbs follow three conjugations; in other words, they can end in three different ways in their infinitive form.

- These conclusions are -ARE, -ERE and –IRE, and they are influenced by verbs conjugated in the various persons.

- Besides these, there are irregular verbs that do not follow a specific rule, but instead, have their own conjugation. Verbs such as "Essere" (to be), "Avere" (to have) and "Andare" (to go) are exceptional cases in which not only the various conjugations' final part changes but also the root itself.

- There are many verbal forms in Italian, even more than in other languages. There are many past verbs like the Simple

Past, the Present Perfect, the Imperfect, and so on. Even the Italians themselves find it difficult to master all of them—that is why it's highly recommended that you start by learning the Present, Past, and Simple Future.

• The Present Perfect is made by taking the verb "to be" or "to have's" present and adding the same present perfect of the verbal form.

• Imperfect is (usually) obtained by adding the suffix -av between the verb's root and its present conclusion.

• The Future and Simple Past both have their own conjugation, which is necessary to learn without any shortcuts.

Altri Modi Verbali (Other Verb Tenses)

The two verbs in this chapter are not the easiest to learn, but luckily, there is good news:

> 1. The verbs are part of the advanced grammar. For this reason, they are not essential during a basic conversation, so you can take all the time you need to learn them.

> 2. The verbs work similarly in both English and Italian, so it will not be as difficult to understand them once the initial difficulties have been overcome.

If the verbs do not fit into a basic conversation, why is it necessary to study them? It is important to know the verbal forms because they compose the hypothetical phrase.

Since, in daily life, you may impose conditions, formulate hypotheses, and talk about the consequences of your actions, you need to know the appropriate verbs to do so.

You will deal with these two verbal forms separately before joining them in the hypothetical phrase, so you'll advance step by step and use a large number of examples to learn the verbs better.

Let's start with the "Congiuntivo" (Subjunctive).

Congiuntivo (Subjunctive)

The subjunctive is every Italian student's nightmare, so much that many Italian speakers are still not able to use this verb correctly and confuse it with the "Condizionale" (Conditional), which is discussed later.

However, this should not worry you: learning to use this verb is not that difficult, just follow some tricks to understand when and where it should be used.

The best use of the subjunctive is in a hypothetical phrase. For this reason, you will use this construction to learn how to use it.

Basically, the subjunctive is a verbal way used in the presence of a "Se" (If) or a "Che" (that).

However, before seeing it within a sentence, let's try to combine it with the various persons.

-ARE verb, "Mangiare" (to eat):

Io mang**i**	I eat
Tu mang**i**	You eat
Lui mang**i**	He eats
Lei mang**i**	She eats
Noi mang**iamo**	We eat
Voi mang**iate**	You eat
Loro mang**ino**	They eat

From this conjugation, it is easy to understand why it is so difficult for Italian people to learn this verb. On the other hand, it is easy to mistake it as the present. Let's make a comparison between them:

Presente Indicativo	Presente Congiuntivo
Io mangi	Io mangio
Tu mangi	**Tu mangi**
Lui mangi	Lui mangia
Lei mangi	Lei mangia
Noi mangiamo	**Noi mangiamo**
Voi mangiate	**Voi mangiate**
Loro mangino	Loro mangiano

As you can see, out of seven persons, three have the same conjugation, and the others just differ in less or one more letter.

The second thing that can be noticed in the translation is that, in English, the subjunctive is not used but replaced by the verb corresponding to the indicative.

It is complex, but combining a verb in -ERE and one in -IRE can help you understand the Italian grammar a little more.

Let's look at the verb "Cadere" (to fall):

Io cada**I** fall	
Tu cad**a**	You fall
Lui cad**a**	He falls
Lei cad**a**	She falls
Noi cad**iamo**	We fall
Voi cad**iate**	You fall
Loro cad**ano**	They fall

As you can see, although it is a bit more complicated, due to the lack of this verb in English, the two verbs work in the same way.

So, let's try a verb that ends in -IRE, like "Nutrire" (to feed):

Io nutr**a**	I feed
Tu nutr**a**	You feed
Lui nutr**a**	He feeds
Lei nutr**a**	She feeds
Noi nutr**iamo**	We feed
Voi nutr**iate**	You feed
Loro nutr**ano**	They feed

The conjugation is very similar in all three cases. What you have seen so far is the present subjunctive. Let's now look at the imperfect subjunctive tense, which is essential to construct your hypothetical phrase.

The English equivalent is the indicative past:

Io nutr**issi**	I fed
Tu nutr**issi**	You fed
Lui nutr**isse**	He fed
Lei nutr**isse**	She fed
Noi nutr**issimo**	We fed
Voi nutr**iste**	You fed
Loro nutr**issero**	They fed

So, here is the difficulty of the verb: as you can see, present and past are quite different from each other. Luckily, once you have learned these two tenses, you will have practically mastered the subjunctive.

Now it is time to look at the Italian conditional and then build your hypothetical phrases.

Il Condizionale (The Conditional)

The conditional is the counterpart of the subjunctive in a hypothetical phrase. It is used to express an action depending on certain conditions.

Unlike the subjunctive, there is a corresponding form in English, and it is the one obtained using "Would".

Let's look at some examples trying to combine the verb "Mangiare" (to eat):

Io mangerei	I would eat
Tu mangeresti	You would eat
Lui mangerebbe	He would eat
Lei mangerebbe	She would eat
Noi mangeremmo	We would eat
Voi mangereste	You would eat
Loro mangerebbero	They would eat

Since an English counterpart of this verb exists, it is easy to understand how it works in Italian.

For example:

Io mangerei la pasta   I would eat the pasta

This is a sentence in which the conditional has been used correctly. What happens if you add a second sentence with the subjunctive?

Il Periodo Ipotetico (The Hypothetical Sentence)

The hypothetical sentence is presented in different forms, and all of them include two sentences: one assumes that an action is taken and the other one requires a condition to be respected. For example:

Mangio la pasta **se** tu la cuoci.   I eat pasta **if** you cook it.

The key behind this hypothetical sentence is the conjunction "If" (Se). Let's see how to correctly formulate this sentence using the subjunctive and the conditional.

The conditional must be used in the sentence that expresses an action under condition:

Mangerei la pasta se…   I would eat pasta if…

The subjunctive is used in the sentence that sets the condition:

…se tu la cuocessi.   …if you cooked it.

Combining these two sentences, you get:

Mangerei la pasta se tu la cuocessi   I would eat pasta if you cooked it.

Obviously, the sentence can be expressed as the opposite:

Se tu cuocessi la pasta, Io la mangerei   If you cooked the pasta, I would eat it

It is unlikely that you will understand these perfectly in just a few sentences, but it was necessary to introduce them so that you can recognize them during your conversations in Italian. With time and practice, you will find yourself using both forms naturally.

To sum up:

- In addition to the indicative, there are two more verbal modes, such as the subjunctive and the conditional.
- The Italian subjunctive does not have a corresponding verbal mode in English, so it is translated using the indicative.
- The subjunctive is often used with the presence of conjunctions like "Che" and "Se" (that and if).
- The Italian conditional corresponds to the English use of "would".
- While expressing a hypothetical sentence, the conditional is often used in one sentence and the subjunctive in another.

Articles

Speaking of sentence construction, the other topic to be discussed is the use of the articles in Italian.

Compared to pronouns and verbs, this field is much easier to understand, but nonetheless, it is necessary to pay attention.

The two main articles are the literal translation of the English ones. As in English, you can find "**a/an**" and "**the**", while in Italian, you find "**un**" e "**il**".

Unfortunately, as you have seen up until now, Italian words tend to change according to the masculine or feminine gender, and the same happens for articles. The article will always have the same gender as their words.

The

Let's start with the determiner article "**the**". In which way is it translated in Italian?

It will be translated as "**IL**" when the following word is masculine:

Il ragazzo.

The boy.

If a feminine word follows the article, it will become "**LA**" instead:

La mamma.

The mother.

Both articles have a plural version, of course. In the masculine's case, it would be "**I**":

I ragazzi.

The boys.

The feminine article becomes "**LE**":

Le mamme.

The mothers.

Quite easy to remember, right? But the explanations are not finished yet because there are two more special cases.

There is another determiner masculine article that has been used with only certain words, "**LO**":

Lo pneumatico.

The tire.

In this particular case, it will only help you with experience and a dictionary, so remember not to be too harsh on yourself since many native-speaking Italians make mistakes and use "**IL**" rather than "**LO**".

So, there is no way of knowing when to use "LO" instead of "IL"? Actually, yes, but it is extremely technical. This article is mainly used with words that start with certain consonants.

What are these?

The masculine words starting with an S and followed by another consonant:

Lo squalo – *The shark*

Lo scontro – *The clash*

Lo spagnolo – *The Spanish*

The masculine words starting with an X, but they are very rare in Italian:

Lo xeno – *The xenon*

Lo xilofono - *The xylophone*

The masculine words starting with Y, but they are also very rare in Italian:

Lo yogurt – *The yogurt*

Masculine words starting with the letter Z, such as:

Lo zabaione – *The eggnog*

Constructed words starting with PS, PN, or GN:

Lo psicologo – *The psychologist*

Lo pneumatico – *The tire*

Lo gnomo – *The gnome*

The plural of "**LO**" become "**GLI**", which follows the same rules listed above.

Another aspect to keep an eye on while talking about determiner articles is that sometimes the feminine article can be replaced by an apostrophe. Not "**LA**", but **L'**. This happens only when the word that follows an article starts with a vowel.

For example:

L'amica. [La amica]

The friend (female).

Even "**LO**" can benefit from this, while still following the same rule:

L'orto. [Lo orto]

The vegetable garden.

When to Use the Definite Article

Now that you have seen different types of definite articles, it is time to learn which cases they should be used in.

1. The first case talks about a specific person. The literal translation of the sentence would be:

Mr. Rossi

è:

Il signor Rossi

The article has been placed before the translation of the word "Mister" since you are talking about a specific person and not a generic "Mister Rossi" you do not know personally.

2. It is the same if you are talking about a lawyer, doctor, or any other professional.

Dr. Bianchi

Il dottor Bianchi

3. The same can be said for continents, nations, and territorial zones (such as islands, mountains, etc.). Here are some examples:

Italy (country)

L'Italia

Europe (continent)

L'Europa

White Mountain (mountain)

Il Monte Bianco

Elba (island)

L'Elba

Toscana (region)

La Toscana

4. The definite article can be used while talking about sports as well:

Football

Il calcio

Basketball

La Pallacanestro

5. Or while talking about languages and the time:

It's three o'clock.

Sono le tre.

English

L'inglese

6. And even while talking about materials, such as:

Gold

L'oro

Cotton

Il cotone

Overall, this is how definite articles work.

A/an

The indefinite article follows more or less the same rules. It starts with a "Un" (a) if followed by a masculine word:

Un cavallo.

A horse.

Then, you use "**Una**" when the following word is feminine:

Una borsa.

A bag.

As for a determiner article, even in this case, you have a second form for the masculine one, which is "**Uno**" and it is used with the same words as "Lo".

Uno squalo.

A shark.

While for a feminine article, in this case, you can have a last letter's elision if there are feminine words. So not "Una" but rather **Un'**.

Un'amica.

A friend (female).

On the contrary, of the determiner article, the masculine "Un" will never get an apostrophe. So, if a word starts with a vowel, the article will simply remain "Un":

Un albero.

A tree.

Let's now see the plural versions. In this case, since "**Uno**" also indicates the first number "**One**", on a plural, it is used as an article that states a higher number, just like you would use the English word "**Some**".

Masculine word "**Dei**":

Un gatto.

A cat.

Dei gatti.

Some cats.

Feminine word "**Delle**":

Delle bambole.

Some dolls.

"**Degli**" for the plural form of "**Uno**":

Degli squali.

Some sharks.

Because of the indefinite article's nature, it also means "One" as a number. The plural version of "Uno" can be replaced with other indefinite adjectives, such as "Alcuni", "Taluni" and "Certi", which can be all translated into the English word: "Some".

To sum up:

- The determiner article "**The**" will be translated in different ways based on the following word's gender (the masculine **Il/Lo** and the feminine **La/L'**) or its number (the plural masculine **I/Gli** and feminine **Le/L'**).

- The indefinite article "**A/an**" will be translated the same, always based on the word's gender (masculine **Un/Uno** and feminine **Una/Un'**) or based on their numbers (masculine **Dei/Degli** and feminine **Delle**).

- The masculine determiner article LO occurs in certain cases only; for example, when the masculine word starts with an X, Z, Y, PS, PN, or GN and the letter S plus another consonant.

- The determiner article is used in some other cases, like: for specific persons, countries, regions, territorial areas, materials, sports, time, and languages.

- The plural form of the indefinite article UN/UNA can be replaced even by indefinite adjectives like "Alcuni", "Taluni" and "Certi". All of them can be translated into "Some".

Numbers

Numbers are almost as important as the alphabet, and they are usually one of the first elements that are explained in each language. And Italian is no exception.

Fortunately, the differences between Italian and English are not many since numbers behave the same way in both languages. They are unique from one to ten, follow a precise rule from eleven to twenty, and then follow a second rule for the rest of the numbers.

Let's start with numbers one to ten:

One	Uno
Two	Due
Three	Tre
Four	Quattro
Five	Cinque
Six	Sei
Seven	Sette
Eight	Otto
Nine	Nove
Ten	Dieci

The numbers of the second decade, up to twenty, in English, follow the rule of -teen. In Italian, there is a similar rule, that of the -dici:

Eleven	Un**dici**
Twelve	Do**dici**
Thir**teen**	Tre**dici**
Four**teen**	Quattor**dici**
Fif**teen**	Quin**dici**
Six**teen**	Se**dici**
Seven**teen**	**Dici**assette
Eigh**teen**	**Dici**otto
Nine**teen**	**Dici**annove
Twenty	Venti

As you can see from this example, from the eleventh to the sixteenth number, the word is made up of the root's number (the first ten) plus the suffix -dici that indicates the tens.

This rule reverses in the last three numbers before reaching the twenty, with the -dici that has been placed at the beginning of the word.

From twenty-one onwards, the numbers are easily understood as they use the root of the ten, just like in English, and the number:

Twenty-one	Ventuno
Twenty-two	**Venti**due
Twenty-three	**Venti**tré
Twenty-four	**Venti**quattro
Twenty-five	**Venti**cinque
etc…	

The first twenty-four numbers are generally the most important because they are the ones that are normally used to define the time of day. By the same principle, to scan minutes and seconds, it is also necessary to know the numbers up to sixty.

Let's now see the tens up to one hundred:

0	Zero	*Zero*
10	Dieci	*Ten*
20	Venti	*Twenty*
30	Trenta	*Thirty*
40	Quaranta	*Forty*
50	Cinquanta	*Fifty*
60	Sessanta	*Sixty*
70	Settanta	*Seventy*
80	Ottanta	*Eighty*
90	Novanta	*Ninety*
100	Cento	*One hundred*

Learning these terms looks more difficult than it is. Except for the first three, from thirty onwards, all the words are made of the base number plus the suffix -ENTA/ANTA.

Curiously, in the Italian tradition, this term also has symbolic value—since the moment a person turns thirty years old, it is usually said as "si entra negli –enta" (*We are in the -enta*), while the moment someone turns forty years old, it is common to say "si entra negli – anta" (*We are in the -anta*).

From 100 onwards, the numbers are extremely easy to remember because they simply take "cento" and add the whole number. Here are some examples:

100 + 6 = 106

| Cento | + | Sei | = | Centosei |

Cento + *Sei* = *Centosei*

100 + 35 = 135

Cento + *Trentacinque* = *Centotrentacinque*

For the other hundreds, it is simpler to enter the corresponding number before the word "cento":

900 **Nove**cento

400 **Quattro**cento

This is up to a thousand. In Italian, the word thousand is written as "Mille" and works exactly like the numbers seen so far.

The only difference between the "Mille" and the "Cento" is that, to formulate the next thousands, it is necessary to put the corresponding number first and then change "Mille" into "Mila":

100   200

Cento   *Due**cento*

1000   2000

Mille   *Due**mila*

The Hour in Italian

When learning a foreign language, being able to ask and communicate the time is one of the first aspects taught, given its great use in everyday life.

Speaking of the hour in Italian, first of all, it is good to remember that Italians use a system of hours different from the "a.m. and p.m." one.

The hours start at 00:00, commonly called "Mezzanotte" (Midnight) and end at 23:59 p.m. (11:59 p.m.); twenty-four hours without being divided between morning and afternoon, using normal numbers. Only noon and midnight have different names.

Here are some examples:

Midnight	Mezzanotte
One a.m.	l'una
Two a.m.	le due
Three a.m.	le tre
Four a.m.	le quattro
Five a.m.	le cinque
Six a.m.	le sei
Seven a.m.	le sette
Eight a.m.	le otto
Nine a.m.	le nove
Ten a.m.	le dieci
Eleven a.m.	le undici
Twelve p.m.	Mezzogiorno

(noon)

As you can see, time is always accompanied by an article in Italian. So, the English sentence:

It's **three** o'clock.

Becomes:

Sono le **tre**.

After noon, the hours take on a double meaning. On the one hand, you see the system based on twenty-four hours:

One p.m.	le tredici
Two p.m.	le quattordici
Three p.m.	le quindici
Four p.m.	le sedici
Five p.m.	le diciassette

Six p.m.	le diciotto
Seven p.m.	le diciannove
Eight p.m.	le venti
Nine p.m.	le ventuno
Ten p.m.	le ventidue
Eleven p.m.	le ventitré

Despite this, in spoken Italian, wide use is made of a division similar to the English one. In this case, the afternoon hours return to be under twelve:

Onep.m.	l'una
Two p.m.	le due
Three p.m.	le tre
Four p.m.	le quattro
Five p.m.	le cinque
Six p.m.	le sei
Seven p.m.	le sette
Eight p.m.	le otto
Nine p.m.	le nove
Ten p.m.	le dieci
Eleven p.m.	le undici

This way of talking about time is very similar to English. For this reason, it is preferable for those approaching Italian from this language. A conversation can, therefore, be:

What time is it?	Che ore sono?
It's three o'clock.	Sono le tre.

And this conversation is fine whether it is three in the morning or the afternoon. But be careful: if the context is missing, it will be necessary to specify the time of day to which that hour refers.

While the hours based on the 24-hour cycle are precise, if you divide the day into two twelve-hour bands, you will have twice the two, three, four and so on.

Since there is no a.m./p.m. formula in Italian, you will have to accompany the time with the time of day:

I woke up at **three a.m.** – Mi sono svegliato alle tre **di notte**

The sentences to be used are, therefore:

Di notte (night)

Di mattina (morning)

Di pomeriggio (afternoon)

Di sera (evening)

As you may have noticed from the previous examples, another difference runs between Italian and English when it comes to time. While in English, the neutral pronoun "it" is always used, in Italian, it is generally replaced with the third person plural.

If it were "They", therefore, you must use the verb: "sono".

The Italian equivalent of "It is", "è", is used only for midnight, noon, and the first hour "l'una".

Half an Hour and a Quarter

So far, precise hours have been discussed, but, of course, you cannot ignore the minutes. It is extremely simple to say the time in Italian, as it is enough to report the hour and minutes using the numbers:

03:21   Sono le **tre e ventuno.**

To these are obviously added the idioms for the quarter of an hour and half an hour.

Here are some direct examples:

It's **a quarter** past three.

Sono le tre e **un quarto**.

It's **a quarter** to three.

Sono le tre meno **un quarto**.

It's **half** past three.

Sono le tre e **mezzo**.

As these are common forms, don't worry too much about it as, in Italy, it is very common to simply say the time using the numbers for the minutes.

Ordinal Numbers

In the previous sections, the cardinal numbers were discussed because they are the most used in the Italian language. Let's now take a look at the ordinal numbers.

In this regard, you will be happy to discover that the functioning of ordinal numbers in Italian is very simple: except for the first ten that are, of course, unique, all others follow the same rule.

First – Primo

Second – Secondo

Third – Terzo

Fourth – Quarto

Fifth – Quinto

Sixth – Sesto

Seventh – Settimo

Eighth – Ottavo

Ninth – Nono

Tenth – Decimo

To obtain most of the other Italian ordinal numbers, it is sufficient to insert "-esimo" at the end of the cardinal number.

Some examples:

Ventuno – Ventun**esimo** (21st)

Trentacinque – Trentacinqu**esimo** (35th)

Diciassette – Diciassett**esimo** (17th)

Unlike the English ordinal numbers, however, the Italian ones are used very rarely.

While ordinal numbers are used in English calendars, cardinal numbers are used in Italian ones.

Here's how the date looks:

The **fifteenth** of December

Il **quindici** dicembre.

Curiously, only the first day of the month is called "Primo" (First), while for all others the normal numbers are used (sometimes the last day of the month is called "Ultimo" (Last)).

For this reason, you will very rarely use ordinal numbers, but it is still good to know them.

One of the few cases in which these numbers are used is when talk about children, to explain which one was born before or after.

In these cases, a word consisting of the ordinal number and the word "genito" (born) is used:

Primogenito

Secondogenito

"Primogenito" therefore literally means "Firstborn".

Money in Italy

Speaking of numbers in Italy, a small paragraph relating to money in this country is included. It is especially useful for those who come from a country that has a different currency than the Euro, such as England (pound) or the United States (dollar).

In fact, as just mentioned, Italy does not have its own currency but uses the single European currency: The Euro.

The currency's value varies continuously over time and during history. It is usually found somewhere between the US dollar and the British pound regarding its purchasing power.

While traveling in Italy, you could find yourself using this currency with cents and banknotes.

The cents are made of eight types, although the use of three of these is starting to be reduced more and more throughout the country.

They are:

1 centesimo (0,01)

2 centesimi (0,02)

5 centesimi (0,05)

10 centesimi (0,10)

20 centesimi (0,20)

50 centesimi (0,50)

1 euro (1,00)

2 euro (2,00)

On the other hand, the banknotes are divided into seven different denominations:

5 euro (5,00)

10 euro (10,00)

20 euro (20,00)

50 euro (50,00)

100 euro (100,00)

200 euro (200,00)

500 euro (500,00)

It is good to know that before implementing the Euro, the old national currency was called "Lira". Its value was clearly inflated, to the point that, at the time of the change, with €500 you could get 1 Million Lire.

This is why, since Italy implemented the Euro, many people are said to be unhappy about this decision that, according to them, has doubled the costs and halved the revenues.

The Lira, although not used anymore, still plays a huge role in contemporary Italian culture, as many people still remember it with nostalgia and expressions that are still in the daily spoken language.

It is not so uncommon to hear Italian people complaining about their economic situations with the expression:

"Non ho una lira." – *"I don't have a lira."*

Before moving on to the final part of this chapter, let's try to insert the various types of numbers into a simulated conversation. This way, you can review how these words are used and learn through conversations in Italian:

A: "Buongiorno, vorrei due biglietti per il treno per Firenze."

A: *"Good morning, I would like two tickets for the train to Florence."*

B: "Ecco a lei; le conviene sbrigarsi: il treno arriva tra cinque minuti.

B: *"Here you are; you should hurry: the train arrives in five minutes."*

A: "Grazie, quanto le devo?"

A: "Thank you, how much do I owe you?"

B: "Sono quindici euro e trenta centesimi."   *B: "It's fifteen euros and thirty cents."*

A: "Accidenti! Non ho una lira! Posso pagare con la carta di credito?"

A: "Damn! I don't have a lira! Can I pay with a credit card?"

B: "Certo, non è il primo cliente con questo problema oggi..."
    B: "Of course, you are not the first customer with this problem today..."

A: "Grazie. Arrivederci!"   *A: "Thank you. Goodbye!"*

B: "Arrivederci!"   *B: "Goodbye!"*

Let's try to see what is interesting in this dialogue. First of all, numbers are widely used. It starts with the customer asking for two tickets to go to Florence. Then it turns out that the train would arrive in five minutes, and costs fifteen euros and thirty cents.

In the end, you also know the way to say "I don't have a lira," so you can see how much is used in spoken Italian.

Finally, an ordinal number was used: the seller said that the customer is not the "primo" (first) to pay with the card.

The conversation you just followed represents a normal exchange between two people. It is easy to understand how knowing the numbers in a given language is important, as they are your key to understanding time, paying, and much more.

To sum up:

- Numbers from 0 to 10 have names to learn.

- Numbers from 11 to 19 gain the suffix (or the prefix) -dici that specify the obtained ten.

- From number 20 onwards, you need to add the minor number next to the ten.

- The number 100 is indicated with the word "Cento". To indicate all subsequent hundreds, simply enter the corresponding number first (example: **Due**cento).

- The number 1,000 is indicated with the word "Mille". In this case, to indicate all the next thousands, it is necessary to insert the corresponding number before and change "Mille" into "Mila" (Es. **Tre**mila).

- Italy uses a time system based on twenty-four hours, but the twelve-hour division is also accepted. For the latter, it is necessary to specify what moment of the day it refers to, stating whether it is morning, afternoon, evening, or night.

- The ordinal numbers are used, usually, to indicate an order of arrival, that is why their use is limited compared to cardinal numbers.

- The Italian currency is the Euro, although there is still some nostalgia towards the old currency (the Lira) that keeps occurring in daily spoken expressions.

Giorni, Mesi e Anni (Days, Months and Years)

The days of the week and months of the year are a necessary field to know when it comes to learning Italian. Moreover, luckily, the months' names are very similar to each other—having the same origin in both English and Italian.

In the next section, you will start from the months and then examine the days of the week—since they have different names compared to the English ones.

I mesi dell'anno (The months of the year)

The calendar used in both English-speaking countries and Italy is the same:

Gennaio	January
Febbraio	February
Marzo	March
Aprile	April
Maggio	May
Giugno	June
Luglio	July
Agosto	August
Settembre	September
Ottobre	October
Novembre	November
Dicembre	December

As you can see, there are small differences in the phonetics of both languages, but they still remain extremely intuitive.

For example, even before translating the list into English, you would have no trouble recognizing which month was "Settembre".

Unfortunately, for the days of the week, it is not so easy.

I giorni della settimana (The days of the week)

The days of the week are taken from celestial bodies and the deities of the country where the language was developed.

While, in Italian, you could find names taken from the Latin deities, in English, the names come directly from Norse gods.

Let's see all of them with their origins:

Lunedì (Luna)	Monday (Moon)
Martedì (Marte)	Tuesday (Tyr)
Mercoledì (Mercurio)	Wednesday (Woden)
Giovedì (Giove)	Thursday (Thor)
Venerdì (Venere)	Friday (Frigg)
Sabato (Saturno)	Saturday (Saturn)
Domenica	Sunday (Sun)

Domenica had the same meaning as in English. In the past, Domenica was called, in Latin, *dies solis*, the day of the sun. With Christianity's influence, it then became *die domini*, the day of the Lord.

Also, here are some day-related words:

Oggi	Today
Ieri	Yesterday
Domani	Tomorrow
Dopodomani	The day after tomorrow
Settimana	Week
Fine settimana	Weekend
Mese	Month
Anno	Year

Greetings

As with every language, the Italian greetings play a fundamental role in your interactions with every Italian person you meet. A correct greeting is your best calling card, and the first step that will decide the direction your conversation will take.

This section of the guide is extremely mnemonic, as it is simply a matter of remembering what greeting should be used in a certain context. For this reason, it is recommended to face it with patience and read the examples provided several times.

Let's start with the most used greetings, "Buongiorno" and "Buonasera". The more generic "Greetings", which, in Italian, is translated as "Salve", is not so commonly used and is often considered outdated in a more natural conversation. For this reason, it is quite easy to understand how to start a conversation based on the time of the day.

Buongiorno, buon pomeriggio, and buonasera.

Learning how to use these greetings is the best way to interact correctly with any person, both in informal and formal environments. "Buongiorno" (Good morning) is used in almost every context, but overall greetings change throughout the day.

"Buongiorno" (Good morning) is used from the early hours of the day to noon;

"Buon pomeriggio" (Good evening) is used from one in the afternoon to five/six in the afternoon; "Buonasera" (Good evening) is used from six in the afternoon onwards; and

"Buonanotte" (Good night) is mostly used to greet someone before going to bed.

A piece of trivia: The word "Buongiorno" has also become famous in the world thanks to the not very natural interpretation of the actor Brad Pitt in the movie *Inglourious Basterds*. The actor greets the Nazi character Hans Landa with "Buongiorno," but he actually used the wrong term—he should have used "Buonasera" since the whole scene is set during the evening.

Now, let's take a look at some greeting examples using the three terms listed above:

Buongiorno, posso avere un caffè?

Good morning, can I have some coffee?

Buon pomeriggio, abbiamo appena finito di pranzare.

Good afternoon, we have just finished lunch.

Buonasera, vorrei un biglietto per Bastardi senza Gloria.

Good evening, I would like a ticket for Inglourious Basterds.

Buonanotte; a domani!

Good night*; see you tomorrow!*

As you can see, these types of greetings are perfect for every context, like with a bartender you just met at the bar or with a friend at the cinema. Even in the workplace and with people with different or higher roles, these kinds of greetings still remain appropriate.

The same cannot be said for one of the most famous greetings in the world: "Ciao", as you will see later.

It is important to notice that the greetings related to the time of the day just talked about can only be used at the beginning of a conversation. Greet a person who is about to leave using "Buongiorno" is incorrect; instead, it is possible to use a similar form that expresses a wish.

In this case, two options are available:

Buona giornata!

Have a nice day!

and

Buona serata!

Have a nice evening!

It is quite easy to understand which of the two terms should be used based on the time of day.

Lastly, although "Buongiorno" is not used at the end of a conversation, it is often used as the only greeting in meeting a person passing through. If you want to briefly greet a person (like on the street, in the office or at school), a simple "Buongiorno", maybe also combined with a smile, is the best and fastest way to convey your greeting.

Ciao and Salve

"Ciao" is one of the most popular Italian greetings, although often used differently than its original meaning.

While greetings like "Buongiorno" and "Buonasera" are only used at the beginning of a conversation, "Ciao" can be used freely, both at the beginning and end of a conversation. "Ciao" remains the same regardless of the time of day, making it the easiest Italian greeting to learn and use.

Despite this, "Ciao" is an informal greeting and can only be used with people you have certain confidence with; otherwise, you risk being disrespectful to others.

A "Ciao" variant already seen is "Salve". It is a more effective and correct greeting that can be used in more formal environments— although it is still recommended to use the greetings above and those related to the times of the day as well.

Let's see a couple of examples with "Ciao" and "Salve":

Ciao, come stai?

Hi, how are you?

Salve, sono qui per un colloquio di lavoro.

Hello, I'm here for a job interview.

Remember: "Hello" cannot be used with people you do not know or whom you are not close enough to allow such an informal greeting.

How to end a conversation

Although this topic has already been examined, there are other ways to end a conversation.

At the end of an informal discussion, "**Ciao**" can be used safely to greet a friend/acquaintance who is leaving. Greeting a person with only "Ciao", however, could turn out to be incomplete if not accompanied by a construction like:

Ciao, alla prossima!

Goodbye, see you soon!

Ciao, ci vediamo presto!

Goodbye, see you soon!

Overall, you can just use "Ciao" as a greeting, but adding a sentence that expresses the wish to see the other person again is a really polite way to end a conversation.

Of course, even in this case, you are talking about informal environments: a friend or acquaintance can both be greeted in this way, but not a stranger or employer. For the latter, a greeting based on the time of the day, like "Buona giornata", turns out to be the best and most polite option.

A very well-known greeting for ending a conversation is also "**Arrivederci**" (See you later), which is slightly less informal than "Ciao" and is the same as "**Ciao**, ci vediamo presto".

Its use is therefore limited only to all those people you know you will meet again. It can, however, also be used in formal environments, as it is more than right to greet a professor or work colleague you will meet again in the future.

If "Arrivederci" can only be used with people you know you will meet again, there is a greeting that is destined for those people you will never meet again: "Addio", a greeting that is rarely used— mostly because of its seriousness that implies you will never meet the person in question again.

"Addio" is especially used for paying respects to a dead person, which means it is the last *ever* greeting towards a person—that is why it is also uncommon in daily Italian language.

Phone greetings

Speaking of greetings at the beginning and end of conversations, you should not ignore telephone calls, an omnipresent element in everyday life. So, how do Italians start and end a phone call?

Luckily, in this case, it is easy to understand how to answer the phone correctly: usually, an Italian who receives a phone call will answer by saying: "**Pronto?**" Its literal translation from Italian to English would be like "Ready?" but it does not make sense as it has no real meaning in Italian either.

The Italian "Pronto?" means, more or less, "Who is it?", and the complete construction is often made of just the sentence: "Hello, who is it?"

While those who receive the call will start the conversation with "Pronto?", the caller will instead interact as if they are both standing in front of each other—so by normally greeting with "Buongiorno/Buona sera/Ciao..." and, of course, telling them who they are.

Even the greetings at the end are the same as a normal conversation, so let's see an example of a typical Italian phone call. In the call, **A** (Andrea), a boy, is calling his girlfriend, **L** (Ljuba), to invite her out to dinner.

A little trivia: Unlike other countries, in Italy, "Andrea" is a mostly male name.

L: "Pronto?"

L: "Hello?"

A: "Ciao, Ljuba, come stai?"

A: "Hi, Ljuba, how are you?"

L: "Andrea! Tutto bene, tu?"

L: "Andrea! All good, how about you?"

A: "Bene. Ti va di andare a mangiare una pizza stasera?"

A: "I'm fine. Do you want to go eat a pizza tonight?

L: "Volentieri! A dopo!"

L: "Gladly! See you later!"

A: "A dopo. Ciao!"

A: "See you later. Bye!"

L: "Ciao!"

L: "Bye!"

In the conversation, you can see several aspects being highlighted during this chapter. The phone call started with a "Pronto?" said by Ljuba, who received the phone call.

After the formalities, "Ciao" was used both at the beginning and end of the conversation, as it allowed in an informal conversation.

Below is a more formal telephone conversation in which you will see the appropriate greetings and way of speaking in this particular circumstance.

The conversation is between **P** (Professor), who calls **S** (Student) on the telephone to communicate their final exam grade:

S: "Pronto?"

S: "Hello?"

P: "Buongiorno, signor Rossi, sono il professor Bianchi."

P: "Good morning, Mr. Rossi, I'm Professor Bianchi."

S: "Buongiorno, professore!"

S: "Good morning, professor!"

P: "La chiamo per comunicarle il risultato dell'esame di matematica. Ha preso 30!"

P: "I called to tell you the result of the math exam. You got 30!"

S: "Grazie, professore! È un'ottima notizia!"

S: "Thank you, professor! It's great news!"

P: "Ottimo lavoro; buona giornata."

P: "Well done; good day."

S: "Grazie; buona giornata a lei!"

S: "Thank you; good day to you too!"

This conversation is slightly more difficult than the others, but let's analyze it step by step. First of all, you can see that the call starts in the same way: "Pronto" is not informal or formal, as it is often not possible to know who is calling.

In this case, no "Ciao" is used as in the previous phone call because a formal conversation has been established between the two since the professor's introduction. You, therefore, find greetings like "Buongiorno" and "Buona giornata", as seen earlier.

It is important to notice that a formal environment, as already seen in the previous chapters, requires the third female person "Lei" instead of the second person "Tu". Always remember this sentence construction, as it is typically Italian and does not exist in English.

A little trivia: If your country has a different grading system, you may not understand what "You got 30!" means. In the Italian university system, the grades range from 0 to 30, where 18 is sufficient, and 30 is the highest grade that can be obtained.

Greetings in E-mails and Mail

Although it is rare to write a letter nowadays, it can still happen. While it is not so rare to write e-mails anymore, this is the most used and common way to communicate in formal environments, such as school or work—hence why it is important to know how to behave during the beginning and end of greetings.

Let's start with a simple example: an informal e-mail. You want to write an email to an Italian friend and show them how fluent you are with their mother language.

How should you start the e-mail?

"Ciao" is the correct way to start an e-message since it is addressed to a friend, such as:

Ciao, Marco,

Come stai? È tanto tempo che non ci sentiamo, così ho deciso di scriverti un'email.

[...]

Hi, Marco,

How are you? It's been so long since our last chat, so I decided to write you an email.

[...]

Another way to start an informal e-mail is by using "**Caro/a**", which is similar to the English word "Dear":

Caro, Marco,

Come stai? Ho saputo che hai iniziato un nuovo lavoro; sono felice per te!

[...]

Dear, Marco,

How are you? I have heard that you have started a new job; I am happy for you!

[...]

Of course, the whole discussion changes if you need to write a more formal email, say addressed to a professor or employer. In addition to the e-mail mode and the use of "Lei", as seen recently, even the initial and final greetings are different from an e-mail exchange between two friends.

The best way to start a formal email is to use the right terms to show others respect. For this reason, the word "**Esimio/a**" (distinguished) or "**Spettabile**" (esteemed) are often used, followed by the recipient's name.

To make it clearer, let's look at two examples. In the first one, you will use an email between a student and a professor, while the second will be between a worker and an employer:

Spettabile Professor Bianchi,

Le scrivo per chiederle maggiori informazioni sull'orario della prossima lezione.

Cordialmente,

Andrea Rossi

Esteemed Professor Bianchi,

I am writing to ask you for more information on the timetable for the next lesson.

With regard,

Andrea Rossi

As you can see, just like in any other language, there is an initial formal construction—in this case, "Dear", and a final one to end the email.

In Italian, the most used closures are:

• Cordialmente (Sincerely) – which expresses cordiality and is aimed at concluding the letter with good manners.

• Distinti saluti (Best regards) – in addition to cordiality, it also transmits a kind of detachment and respect towards the other.

As seen in the previous example, the Italian third female person is always mandatory in this case too:

Le *scrivo per chiederle maggiori informazioni [...]*

As stated before and to make it clearer, let's look at an example in a working environment:

Esimio Dottor Favilli,

Con la presente le comunico la mia adesione al seminario di questo fine settimana.

Distinti saluti,

Andrea Rossi

Distinguished Dr. Favilli,

I hereby inform you of my adhesion to this weekend's seminar.

With best regards,

Andrea Rossi

Final Greetings

Here are a couple of common greetings used in daily Italian language and conversations:

Ci vediamo domani – See you tomorrow

Piacere di conoscerti – Nice to meet you

Ci vediamo presto – See you soon

Alla prossima – Until next time

To sum up:

- There are two kinds of greetings. The first one is based on the time of the day and is used in both formal and informal environments (**Buongiorno, Buon pomeriggio,** and **Buona sera**). The second one (**Ciao**) is only used in informal environments but is still not influenced by the time of the day.

- An informal and similar word like "**Ciao**" is "**Salve**"—less used than the first one but still correct in spoken Italian.

- "**Ciao**" can be used both at the beginning and the end of a conversation. "**Salve**" can be only used at the beginning, as like "**Buongiorno**", "**Buon pomeriggio**", and "**Buona sera**".

- To end a conversation with the latter, it is common to use a form of a wish, such as: "**Buona giornata/serata**".

- "**Arrivederci**" is a greeting that can only be used while ending a conversation, and only if it is expected that you will meet the person again.

- "**Addio**" is a greeting used at the end of a conversation and only to people you are sure not to meet again.

- An Italian answering the phone will always say "**Pronto?**", so the rules regarding greetings will follow the same rules as an eye to eye conversation.

- There are several ways to start an e-mail. If it is informal, it's possible to use "**Ciao**" and "**Caro/a**" followed by the recipient's name.

- If the e-mail is a formal one, the names will be "**Spettabile**", "**Esimio**", and "**Gentile**".

- The closure greetings in both letters and e-mails are, usually, "**Cordialmente**" or "**Distinti saluti**".

Frasi Comuni In Italiano (Basic Italian sentences)

Before going too deep into the Italian language, in order to be able to speak about your life, school, and work, let's summarize what you have seen so far. In this chapter, a series of basic Italian sentences are listed that will come in handy.

In this particular case, you will see sentences composed (usually) of one to five words that are included in the basic Italian.

Let's get started with:

Thank you – Grazie

You have already seen how it is possible to express gratitude in Italian and how to apologize. In this chapter, in addition to refreshing your memory on words you have already learned, you will also take a look at more complex constructions. As an example, while "Grazie" expresses gratitude, you may feel so grateful that a simple "Grazie" is not enough.

In English, you would use "Thank you very much", but in Italian?

Thank you very much – Grazie mille

The literal translation of this expression is "Thanks one thousand," which, like many other literally translated sentences, does not make any sense.

"Grazie mille" is the shortened version of "Grazie mille volte", so that would be translated into "Thank you one thousand times."

Some other guides dedicated to learning Italian show an alternative translation, "Grazie tante".

Although the translation is correct, this sentence is often used sarcastically, and for this reason, it is far from a true grateful feeling.

"Grazie mille" is used much more widely in daily spoken Italian.

You're welcome – Prego

For responding to "Grazie", Italian uses the expression "Prego" (literally "I pray") just as "You're welcome" is used in English.

The word "Prego", however, is also used in another context: when you hold the door for someone, or while handing out an object to someone, you can still say, "Prego."

Please – Per favore

"Per favore", just like its English counterpart, is an expression used for asking a courtesy from someone you are talking to. Its literal meaning would be something like "Do me a favor", but, of course, it is simply a common construction in spoken Italian.

There is a variation to this answer: "Per piacere", which has the same meaning (even if it is used, usually, in more informal environments)

Yes – Sì

The definitive positive answer.

No – No

This is probably one of the easiest words to remember, but keep in mind how the letter O is pronounced in Italian rather than in English.

Excuse me?/Pardon me? – Mi scusi?

A cordial expression for asking permission. There is a more informal version used when, for example, you need to walk through a crowded place. In this case, it is said: "Permesso."

I'm sorry – Mi dispiace

The most used word for expressing sorrow. This sentence has already been explained in the dedicated chapter, and that is why it is not going to be examined in depth now. However, it is worth adding that if you are going to show grief over the death of a person to someone, then you must use the word "Condoglianze" (My condolences).

I don't understand – Non capisco

Usually, this sentence is compared to the previous one in order to say sorry for not understanding a certain thing.

I don't speak Italian – Non parlo italiano

A very useful sentence to use at the beginning of your journey through learning Italian. Another good and useful alternative to this is: "Sto imparando l'italiano" (I am learning Italian).

I don't speak Italian very well – Non parlo molto bene l'italiano

As you can see, the Italian language is mostly anticipated by the article. The article can be added in the previous sentence, but only in the case that it can be eliminated to make it shorter.

If this confuses you, always use the article.

Do you speak English? – Parla Inglese?

The third-person singular (Lei parla) is used because it is a sentence often used while talking to a stranger (perhaps for asking directions). If, instead, you are asking it to a friend or family member, you can use the second person: "Parli Inglese?"

Speak slowly, please – Parli piano, per favore

Even in this case, you can apply the same rule as before.

Repeat, please – Ripeta, per favore

The sentence is correct and is the best to use if you have not mastered the language yet. However, it lacks courtesy, so it would be better to put the sentence this way:

Mi scusi, può ripetere? – Excuse me, could you repeat, please?

What's your name? – Come ti chiami?

You already saw both the verb and the names.

How are you? – Come stai?

This is the most basic sentence to ask about someone's health. If you want to ask how life is going or just as a courtesy to someone, you can use the sentence: "Come va?" instead.

In addition to these basic sentences, there are a variety of idioms and proverbs typical of the Italian language that you might not understand if you have not heard them before. For this reason, in the last chapters of the book, this specific topic will be of focus, offering you the third and also the last point of in-depth analysis of Italian words right after the vocabulary and this one dedicated to basic sentences.

About Me

After seeing the most common use of many Italian expressions, it is time to start talking about you. The ability to introduce yourself and make yourself known is essential in every language: people want to know who you are before opening themselves up to you.

This chapter will focus on personal information and how it is possible to talk about yourself and ask others something.

The Name

Naturally, you will have to introduce yourself once you arrive in Italy. In Italian, there are two ways of saying one's name.

The first is the most literal but least smooth way to do it and is also the easiest to use for an English speaker since it is the direct translation of the English construction.

In English, you would present yourself as:

"My name is Paolo."

This sentence makes perfect sense in Italian as well, and it is expressed by:

"Il mio nome è Paolo."

Let's analyze each word of the sentence:

Il (as you saw in the first chapters, the article is essential in Italian)

Mio (first-person possessive pronoun, the equivalent of "my")

Nome (noun, direct translation of "name")

È (the verb essere – "to be", third-person singular and translation of "is")

Paolo (name)

Clear, right? Actually, this is a very technical construction, and you will hardly hear an Italian saying their name in this way. Usually, only three words are used in Italian:

"Mi chiamo Paolo."

The direct translation of this sentence would be: "I call myself Paolo", but it doesn't make any sense.

Let's reanalyze the sentence:

Mi (third-person singular, a reflexive pronoun, and the direct translation of "myself")

Chiamo (verb, first-person singular of verb "chiamare" – "to call")

Paolo (name)

The first construction you have read is also correct, but a shorter version and construction often replace it:

"Sono Paolo."

In this case, there are only two words:

Io (implied subject, typical in Italy as seen earlier – "I")

Sono (the verb "to be", first-person singular – "am")

Paolo (name)

The last name doesn't usually follow any specific rules, and it is introduced with the name while it's hardly used in a conversation. Curiously, based on different Italy's regions, the last name can replace the name during a conversation, and the article precedes it.

Example:

Paolo Bianchi

Usual case – "Lui è **Paolo**" (using the name)

Regional case – "Lui è **il Bianchi**" (using the last name)

Do not worry too much about this variation, though, because it is really informal and restricted to certain Italian regions.

However, while introducing yourself, you must remember another word: "Piacere". This word is the short version of "Piacere di conoscerti" (Nice to meet you) and is always used during the first meeting between two people.

When this pronoun is used, the sentence could be shortened even more to using only the name.

Instead of:

"Sono Paolo."

You will get:

"Piacere, Paolo."

Let's look at a more focused example to understand better what is explained above.

Example of Paolo and Luca who are talking while meeting for the first time:

Paolo: "Ciao, io sono Paolo."

Paolo: "Hi, I'm Paolo."

Luca: "Ciao, Paolo, io sono Luca."

Luca: "Hi, Paolo, I'm Luca."

The same interactions while using "Piacere di conoscerti":

Paolo: "Ciao, io sono Paolo."

Paolo: "Hi, I'm Paolo."

Luca: *"Piacere di conoscerti, Luca."*

Luca: *"Nice to meet you, Luca."*

However, as stated before, the sentence "Piacere di conoscerti" is shortened to "Piacere" most of the time:

Paolo: *"Ciao, io sono Paolo."*

Paolo: *"Hi, I'm Paolo."*

Luca: *"Piacere, Luca."*

Luca: *"Nice ~~to meet you~~, Luca."*

It is implied that during this conversation, both gave each other a handshake, which is a current gesture during first meetings in Italy.

The sentences to remember related to this context are:

- *"Come ti chiami?" – "What's your name?"*
- *"Qual è il tuo cognome?" – "What's your last name?"*

I'm From...

Another common piece of information to provide while introducing yourself is your home country, and

there are different ways to say this. One is the almost direct translation from English: "I am from..."; although there are some differences.

In Italian, the sentence used is:

"Sono di Roma."

Let's reexamine the sentence word by word:

Io *(implied subject – "I")*

Sono *(verb to be, first-person singular – "am")*

Di *(preposition, belonging complement – "of")*

Roma *(city)*

In the Italian sentence, the city where they are from is not specified, like in the English sentence; rather, it is specified as belonging to that city, as like they were part of it.

This is the most common form to find during an introduction. Between these, you find a similar sentence to the English one:

"Vengo da Roma." – *I come from Rome* (literal translation).

"Sono nato a Roma." – *I was born in Rome.*

Eventually, it is common to get a reply with an adjective after asking about the birthplace. So, instead of saying:

"Io sono di Roma." – *I am of Rome.*

They could say:

"Sono romano." – *I am Roman.*

While talking about your home country, another very common and useful word is the English translation of "mother tongue". As in English, the Italian word indicates being perfectly fluent in a certain language, so that means a literal translation.

The Italian word is "madrelingua" where "madre" means "mother" and "lingua" means "tongue". The only difference between Italian and English is that, in the first case, the words are combined, while in English, they are not.

I Live In…

You have seen the past explored; now, it is necessary to talk about the present, and then explain where your current home is. Before seeing the various sentences, it is worth highlighting that, in Italian, two words can indicate the act of "living somewhere".

The first one is the verb "to live", as is the same in English. The sentence is:

"I live in Rome."

And the literal translation is:

"Io vivo a Roma."

The literal English translation may be helpful in order to use the verb "to live" as it is perfectly acceptable in spoken Italian.

In Italian, however, you will often hear another term that has the same meaning: "Abitare".

While "Vivere" overall means "Being alive", and its meaning is used within the context of "Living in a place", "Abitare" only means "Living in one place". For this reason, it is a more precise term than "Vivere", but it is not necessarily the only correct way to use it.

That is why the sentence:

"I live in Rome."

Can be translated into:

"Io vivo a Roma."

And also as:

"Io abito a Roma."

And both options listed above are correct.

The sentence changes slightly if, instead of saying only the city, you will mention the state or the address where you are staying. Nonetheless, in both cases, you will not have to use the preposition "a" but the "in" preposition.

Here are some direct examples:

I live in Rome – Io vivo **a** Roma

I live in Italy – Io vivo **in** Italia

I live in Giovanni Gianni street, 43 – Io vivo **in** Via Giovanni Gianni, 43

This is a little difference that it is useful to remember in order to speak Italian correctly.

Pet

Another important aspect of many people's lives, other than being a great conversation topic, is pets. Many people have a dog or a cat, and how can you talk about them? First of all, it is worth knowing the different animals' names.

Here are some examples:

- Dog   –   Cane
- Cat   –   Gatto
- Mouse   –   Topo
- Snake   –   Serpente
- Hamster   –   Criceto
- Bunny   –   Coniglio
- Parrot   –   Pappagallo
- Ferret   –   Furetto
- Fish   –   Pesce
- Goldfish   –   Pesce rosso

A little trivia: "Goldfish" is translated as "Pesce rosso", which literally means "Red fish".

As previously mentioned, there is not a neutral gender in Italian, so that is why when you are talking about your pets, you will have to refer to them with their gender.

I'm Going Out Tonight

During previous chapters and sections, there were many examples of how to correctly behave in a working environment. However, it is also true that there is more to life than just work!

Let's look at some words that can be useful while talking about enjoyable events:

- Cinema – Cinema

The word is the same as in Italian, but the pronunciation is different. The first part, "Ci-", is pronounced like the "Ch-" in the English word "Cheetah".

- Restaurant – Ristorante
- Pizzeria – Pizzeria
- Bar – Bar
- Pub – Pub

As you can see, luckily, many Italian and English words have been influenced by each other—that is why they are the same or easy to remember.

When referring to nights out, the Italian verb for that is the same as the English language: "Uscire" (to go out), and in this case, it is quite easy to use too.

Curiously, the verb "Prendere" is also similar to the English "Pick up"—although the literal meaning is slightly different, the application is the same.

Let's see some sentences that use both verbs:

*Stasera esci? – Are you **going out** tonight?*

*Ti passo **a prendere** alle sei. – **I'll pick** you up at six.*

In the second sentence, it is important to notice two things. The first is the verbal form application in this sentence: even if you are talking about the future, and, in English, it uses "will" for the same purpose, in Italian, it can be used in a very natural way—in the present instead.

This, of course, is if you are talking about a very close present.

If you are talking about months instead:

Ti passerò a prendere il dieci gennaio. – I'll pick you up on January 10.

Another thing that could be noticed in the example is that, even though the verbal form is similar, the Italian verb "Prendere" is always combined with another verb like "Passare" (to pass) or "Venire" (to come).

If we recheck the sentence:

Ti passo a prendere alle sei.

And split it word for word:

Io (sentence implied subject – "I")

Ti (second-person singular pronoun – "You")

Passo (first-person singular of the verb "Passare" – "Pass")

A prendere (the infinitive verb "Prendere" – "to pick up")

Alle sei (time – "at six")

The sentence could be a little confusing because of the pronoun's position "**Ti**", but as you have already seen in the chapter about this sentence's part, the pronoun can be moved to many points of the sentence.

It can be moved next to the verb (but the sentence would be too complex):

*(Io) passo a prendere **te** alle sei. – I'll pass to pick you up at six.*

Although written like this, it is much similar to the English structure and is too forced/unnatural.

The most used version in spoken Italian is the one united with the verb itself:

*(Io) passo a prende**rti** alle sei.*

Let's see some useful sentences for planning a night out:

- Do you want to go out with me? – **Ti va di uscire con me?**
- Do you want to go to the cinema tonight? – **Vuoi andare al cinema stasera?**

Remember that in the informal environments, usually, you can reduce everything to just a few simple words. This subject cannot be explained too much in this guide because these shortcuts are based on how much you could be familiar with a person, but you can still say:

Pizza, stasera? – *Pizza, tonight?*

The sentence, without verbs and subjects, still makes sense in a familiar environment—that is why, as much as it is important to learn more words and be fluent in Italian, remember that *experience* is really helpful to overcome difficult times while learning the language.

The Birthday

This is a topic discussed often but shows differences between English and Italian.

The most important difference is the word used to point to the moment of birth, which is a very subtle difference:

I was born on 21 April 1992

Io sono nato il 21 Aprile 1992

The main difference between the two verbs, both English and Italian, is that the English one is used as a passive form. "I was born" states that, in that certain moment or even place, *I* have been born from my mother.

In Italian, however, the verb shows a more active form and states the birth itself as an action.

It is not so important when it comes to learning Italian, but still, it is an interesting curiosity worth knowing.

For this reason, the literal translation is almost used (as you can see from the number of words) from the English.

If you want to say just the birthday instead, it will be enough to say:

My birthday is April 21

Il mio compleanno è il 21 Aprile

There is still a little difference compared to English while saying your age.

In English, there are usually two different ways:

I'm twenty-seven

or

I'm twenty-seven years old.

In Italian, there is a word in the middle of the two. It is not enough to say only the number; it has to come with the word "anni" (years):

Io ho ventisette anni

It must be noticed that the verb "to have", in Italian, "Io ho" (I have) is used, while in English, the verb "to be", "I'm/ I am" is used.

The classic birthday song has the same origins, both in the English and Italian versions, so you are talking about a literal translation:

Happy birthday to you

Happy birthday to you

Happy birthday dear [NAME]

Happy birthday to you

«Tanti auguri a te

tanti auguri a te

tanti auguri a [NOME]

tanti auguri a te»

A little trivia: During a birthday, you may hear the sentence "Cento di questi giorni" (one hundred of these days). This sentence is a wish of long life and is very common among Italian traditions: wishing for hundreds of these days (birthdays), is wishing for many other hundreds of years of life to the guest of honor.

There is another word that is very common while talking about birthdays: the verb "Compiere" (to do), which is used to communicate the day of birth in an active form.

For example:

Oggi compio gli anni.

And its literal translation is:

Today I do my years.

Which does make sense.

The translation based on that meaning is:

Oggi è il mio compleanno.

It may be way more complicated to understand than other literal translations you have already seen, but you could hear this construction while talking to an Italian person.

Now, let's take a step back and look at a conversation that uses the information provided in this chapter:

A: **"Buongiorno. Sto cercando un libro per il mio compleanno."**

A: "Good morning. I'm looking for a book for my birthday."

B: **"Buongiorno. Vediamo se posso aiutarla. Come si chiama?"**

B: "Hello. Let's see if I can help you. What's the name?"

A: **"Si chiama… "Il Sentiero dei Nidi di Ragno", di Italo Calvino."**

A: "It's called … *The Path of the Spider's Nest*, by Italo Calvino."

B: **"Intendevo lei: come si chiama?"**

B: "I meant you: what's your name?"

A: **"Mi scusi. Mi chiamo Antonio, e lei?"**

A: "Sorry. My name is Antonio, and you?"

B: **"Barbara… Vediamo di trovare questo libro..."**

B: "Barbara ... Let's find this book ..."

A: **"Grazie. Vengo da un paesino, e non sono abituato a queste librerie gigantesche!"**

A: "Thanks. I'm from a small town, and I'm not used to these gigantic bookstores!"

B: **"E come facevi a leggere?"**

B: "And how did you read?"

A: **"Avevo qualche libro, ma il mio coniglio se li è mangiati."**

A: "I had some books, but my rabbit ate them."

B: **"Davvero? Allora questo è un regalo per il suo coniglio!"**

B: "Really? Then this is a gift for your rabbit!"

A: **"No, oggi è il mio compleanno; il suo è ancora lontano!"**

A: "No, today is my birthday; his birthday is still far away!"

To sum up:

- Saying your name in Italian uses two different verbal forms, such as the verb "essere" (to be) and the verb "chiamare" (to call).
- Stating your home country also uses two different verbal forms: the verb "essere" (to be), which states belonging to a certain city or nation, and the verb "venire" (to come).
- Stating where you currently live uses the verb "vivere" (to live) or the more specific verb "abitare".
- Speaking about a very near future uses the present instead of the future.
- Speaking about birth uses the passive verb in English, while in Italian, it uses an active verbal form.

Leisure and Art

It is not possible not to talk about this topic as Italy offers so much in the way of art and entertainment. Life is not just made up of work and study—as important as these are. For this reason, you will now learn some typical phrases that can be used in this context.

Cinema and Television

One of the most common phrases about cinema is:

"Il mio film preferito è..." – "My favorite movie is..."

As you can see, the construction of the sentence is very similar, both in English and in Italian, so what is there to know about the world of cinema, as far as Italy is concerned?

• The theaters – Despite its profound theatrical history, the average Italian rarely goes to the theater to see shows, which is why many theaters are also used as cinemas. The term "Teatro" (theater), therefore, indicates the place where it is usually possible to watch live comedies and tragedies.

• Cinema – You have already seen in previous chapters how the word "Cinema" is pronounced. Speaking of cinema, you can also hear the word "Multisala" (Multiplex), which is a particular type of cinema in which different films are projected in different rooms at the same time.

When talking about films with an Italian person, it might surprise you to discover that doubling the films that come from abroad is a fundamental part of Italian culture.

Watching a film in the original language, in fact, is a custom that has caught on only in the last few years—thanks to the advent of the internet—, but despite this, many Italians watch movies only if they have been translated and dubbed in their language.

The Italian dubbing school is among the best in the world and is a source of pride for many enthusiasts in the sector. For this reason, the realization that an Italian has of a movie is fundamentally different from one of the spectators in the original country of that film—an aspect to take into consideration when you talk about movies.

Another question linked to the world of cinema is:

"Chi è il tuo attore preferito?" – "Who is your favorite actor?"

And a shared phrase:

"Era un film bellissimo; mi sono commosso/a" – "It was a great movie; I was moved."

Knowing that all the movies that are broadcast in Italy have been redubbed in Italian could upset you, but don't worry—there is good news in this regard.

Firstly, in doing so, you have at your disposal a huge number of films in Italian that you can use as material to improve your knowledge and pronunciation of the language. Almost all movies of big productions enjoy a masterful dubbing, so try searching for your favorite dubbed movie in Italian.

Secondly, if you are in Italy and wish to see a film in the original language, always remember that many multiplexes offer screenings in the original language.

Let's see how you can ask about it:

"Il film con Tom Hanks è in Inglese?" – "Is the movie with Tom Hanks in English?"

Often it will be enough to ask directly at the cinema box (or you can y search on the internet).

Other phrases that can be useful in this context:

"L'ho già visto" – "I've already seen it."

"È sottotitolato in Inglese?" – "Is it subtitled in English?"

"Ci sarà un intervallo?" – "Will there be an interval?

The final question can already be answered in this guide: most Italian cinemas have removed the interval from their projections, even if it is not a written rule.

Other words to know about this topic:

Film	–	Movie
Attore	–	Actor
Attrice	–	Actress
Regista–		Movie director
Sceneggiatore –		Screenwriter
Commedia	–	Comedy
Tragedia	–	Tragedy
Sottotitoli	–	Subtitles
La prima	–	Premiere

In this case, the Italian term literally means "The first" and refers to the first screening of the film in question.

Fila	–	Queue
Corto	–	Short film
Fine	–	The end

Trama –   Plot

To these words are also added all those that are inherent to the genre of the film, such as:

Azione   –   Action

Orrore/Paura   –   Horror

Guerra   –   War

Romantico/D'amore –   Romantic/Love

Fantascienza   –   Science fiction

And many other words, even more specific about this world. Maybe you would like to express an opinion after seeing the movie.

First, is the standard phrase:

"Il film era..." – "The movie was…"

At this point, you can add what you thought of the movie while watching it. Here are some common terms:

Avvincente   –   Gripping

Veloce   –   Fast-moving

Noioso   –   Boring

Terribile   –   Awful

Pauroso   –   Scary

Triste   –   Sad

Brutto   –   Bad

But, of course, art is not limited to just the big screen. There are many other areas where you can practice your Italian.

La Musica / The Music

Music often gets to us on a personal level, as many people usually play a musical instrument. For this reason, it is possible to talk about this topic from different points of view.

From a listener's point of view, a common question is:

- **Ti piace la musica?** – Do you like music?

If you were asked this question, the answers you could give are:

- **Mi piace la musica.** – I like music.
- **Non mi piace la musica.** – I don't like music.

If the topic develops further, it is possible to go into more detail by asking what kind of music a person likes to listen to. Fortunately, at least concerning the musical genres born in countries beyond the Alps, the name remains the same.

Here are some direct examples to consolidate the concept:

Musica Pop   –   Pop Music

Musica Rock   –   Rock Music

Musica Metal –   Metal Music

And so on.

The two questions generally asked about music are:

-    **Chi è il tuo cantante preferito?** – Who's your favorite singer?
-    **Qual è la tua band preferita?** – What is your favorite band?

You will discover that Italians, while carrying a famous musical tradition, greatly appreciate foreign music, and, in this case, you don't have to worry about the songs being translated.

The field of music, in this sense, has remained untainted.

However, if your passion for music has led you to play a musical instrument, you may want to know what the various instruments are called:

Chitarra   –   Guitar

Pianoforte	–	Piano
Violino	–	Violin
Batteria	–	Drums
Flauto	–	Flute
Basso	–	Bass
Tromba	–	Trumpet

Curiously, while the names of some instruments remain similar both in English and in Italian (as in the case of the violin), there are other instruments whose name is very different from the English version.

An example is "Batteria" (drums) whose name literally indicates the electric battery used, for example, in machines.

La Pittura e La Scultura / Painting and Sculpture

Painting in Italy is a fundamental part of its past, thanks to the masterpieces born before, during, and after the Renaissance.

There is a reason why Italy is considered one of the countries of art par excellence, and painting and sculpture (of which will be discussed shortly) play a fundamental role in this artistic tradition.

Let's look at some useful phrases and terms to use in this context:

"Dove è il museo più vicino?" – "Where is the closest museum?"

"Mi piace quel pittore!" – "I like that painter!"

"Voglio andare a vedere quella mostra." – "I want to go see that exhibition."

Even more important is to know all the terms that can be used within these sentences. Here are the most common words when speaking of an artistic environment:

Il quadro	–	The painting
Il pittore	–	The painter

L'affresco	–	Fresco
Il pennello	–	Brush
La mostra	–	Exhibition
Il Rinascimento	–	The Renaissance
Il Medio Evo	–	Middle Ages
La scultura	–	Sculpture
La galleria	–	Gallery
Asta	–	Auction
Guida	–	Guide

Let's imagine you are at an exhibition. The questions that might be useful to know are:

"Posso scattare una fotografia al quadro?" – "Can I take a picture of the painting?"

This is a more than legitimate question to learn, as in many galleries, it is forbidden to take photographs of the works on display—even more so if the flash is used during photography, so it is important also to ask:

"Posso usare il flash?" – "Can I use the flash?"

Fortunately, as far as these small details are concerned, if you are visiting a museum or exhibition, it will always be specified on various signs.

To conclude this chapter, let's look at a conversation between two people with an artistic theme, where you will make extensive use of the sentences you have seen so far and the specific terms of this field:

A) **"Che facciamo questa sera?"**
A) "What are we going to do tonight?"
B) **"Non saprei. Hai qualche idea?"**
B) "I don't know. Do you have any ideas?"

A)   **"Potremmo andare al cinema. Stasera c'è quel nuovo film…"**

A) "We could go to the cinema. Tonight there is that new movie..."

B)   **"Quale? Quello con Will Smith come protagonista?"**

B) "What? The one with Will Smith as the protagonist?"

A)   **"No, il film animato scritto da Spielberg."**

A) "No, the animated movie written by Spielberg."

B)   **"Ah, no. L'ho già visto."**

B) "Ah, no. I have already seen it."

A)   **"Okay, che ne dici di andare ad ascoltareun gruppo musicale?"**

A) "Okay, how about going to listen to a band?"

B)   **"Quale gruppo?"**

B) "Which band?"

A)   **"Si chiamano Tenacious B. Li conosci?"**

A) "They are called Tenacious B. Do you know them?"

B)   **"Sì, ma non abbiamo i biglietti!"**

B) "Yes, but we don't have the tickets!"

A)   **"Hai ragione… Che ne dici di andare a vedere la mostra di Magritte allora?"**

A) "You're right... How about going to see Magritte's exhibition then?"

B)   **"Un'esibizione con i suoi quadri? Certo!"**

B) "An exhibition with his paintings? Sure!"

As you can see, it is quite simple to communicate in Italian about art: all you have to do is remember the correct words!

To sum up:

• In the Italian tradition, all foreign films (or at least those that reach Italian soil) are dubbed by overwriting the original language. Although it is, therefore, more difficult to watch a film in English in an Italian cinema, this also gives you a great opportunity to learn Italian by watching your favorite movies redubbed in the language.

Indicazioni (Directions)

While visiting Italy for the first time, it is important to know how to move around and ask for directions to visit places. To do this, it is good to know the typical expressions and how the road system works.

Unlike other countries in the world, the so-called neighborhoods in Italy are quite uncommon. Each city or town is divided into "Vie" (Streets) and "Piazze" (Town Squares), with a further subdivision for each building within it. Because of this, there are the "Numeri civici" (house numbers) to identify the various buildings in a certain city area.

In an Italian "via", usually, even numbers and odd numbers are placed on buildings in front of each other (so not on the same line) and in numerical order.

Here's an example: while entering "Via San Marco", you find on your left the street number 1, and on the right the street number 2. Continuing along the road, then, on the left, you see the numbers 3, 5, 7, 9, 11, 13... while on the right, you see the numbers 4, 6, 8, 10, 12, 14... and so on. Naturally, the order of the numbers can be increasing or decreasing, based on the direction from which you arrive.

Sometimes, these numbers may have a further division based on letters, so it is possible to find "numeri civici" like 1A, 1B, 1C and so on.

These numbers are also present in "Piazze" and the "Periferia" (suburbs area).

Before seeing some useful sentences to help you reach your destination, you have to learn how to ask information for reaching that destination. All the nouns in the vocabulary section have also been reported to let you check them quickly in the future.

Come Chiedere Informazioni? (How To Ask For Directions?)

If you want to arrive at a certain destination, you should ask directions correctly. In this section, you will also see some places of interest, but for now, let's start with the basic questions.

If you already know where to go, you should ask:

"Mi scusi. Sto cercando il Duomo, può aiutarmi?"

"Excuse me. I'm looking for the Duomo, can you help me?"

Let's analyze this sentence word by word:

Mi Scusi – It is easy to remember since it sounds like a reversed *Excuse me*. Remember always to use the third-person feminine with a person you do not know.

(Io) – Implied subject, *I*

Sto cercando – *am looking for*

Il Duomo – *The Duomo*

Può – *Can you*, in this case (Lei); it is also an implied subject

Aiutarmi – *Help me*, as you have already seen in the first chapters of the book, sometimes the particle "me" can be added to the verb.

This elision can be confusing for non-Italian speakers, but let's try to see how the sentence would be if the particle "me" weren't combined and with the presence of the subjects:

Mi scusi, Io sto cercando il Duomo. Lei può aiutarmi?

Excuse me, I'm looking for the Duomo. Can you help me?

In this case, the construction of the sentence is similar to English. Feel free to use this version if you find it easier to remember—it is correct even if it sounds a bit unnatural.

Let's see some other examples:

Sto cercando un ristorante. Può aiutarmi?

I'm looking for a restaurant. Can you help me?

Sto cercando un bagno. Può aiutarmi?

I'm looking for a bathroom. Can you help me?

Sto cercando la stazione. Può aiutarmi?

I'm looking for the train station. Can you help me?

After practicing asking for directions, you will have to learn the names of places you are interested in. Some places of interest are listed in the vocabulary within the first part of the book, but do not worry: now you will see some of the most common places in Italy with their description.

Punti di Interesse (Places of Interest)

- **Ospedale** – *Hospital*

This is, unfortunately, one of the most important places to reach, both while visiting Italy during holidays and while living in this country. The Italian healthcare system is public, although some additional costs may be applied in some cases.

The whole building is made of different medical divisions and the "Pronto Soccorso" (emergency room). In the Pronto soccorso, every patient is labeled with a different color code based on how severe their health conditions are.

- **Bar** – *Cafè*

The bar is the ideal destination for any refreshment break during your strolls through the Italian streets. In an Italian bar, it is possible, in general, to find sandwiches and desserts, as well as drinks and the famous Italian espresso.

This topic is discussed in more detail later, in the chapter dedicated to Italian food. Now you are going to talk more about the Bar itself.

Italian culture does not foresee the widespread presence of stores like Starbucks—although these are being born in the largest cities of the country, are often tainted by Italian tastes, and are so different from their American counterparts.

Italians are not used to coffee houses since people are more willing to drink coffee quickly rather than sit in a bar for several hours while working, for example. Anyway, they are rare and located in the largest cities.

There are two different kinds of bars usually more frequented during the evening:

The first one is the "Pub", which, as you can see, does not need an English translation since the meaning is the same. In a typical British pub, you can enjoy different types of alcoholic drinks (especially beers) with music in the background. These kind of pubs are for those who want a relaxing evening rather than dancing in a more crowded place like the Discoteca (Disco).

The second one is the "Paninoteca" (Sandwich place), and as the name suggests, it is a place where you can buy different kinds of sandwiches.

The Paninoteca is usually compared to fast food, although they distance themselves from true fast-food chains like McDonald's or Burger King for their more typical Italian food. However, fast-food chains, such as McDonald's, are very popular among Italian people, especially the youngsters, but their menu is completely different from other fast-food chains in order to meet Italian taste.

- **Ristorante** – *Restaurant*

Speaking of "Slow food", instead, the Ristorante (restaurant) is the most common and famous place to eat Italian food. In this kind of place, it is possible to sit and eat calmly. Actually, in Italy, there are not just Ristoranti but two other kinds of places to eat:

steria – The word "Osteria" (Tavern) meets its origin within the common people and dates back to ancient times—although today they have changed into a more modern type of osteria. What is the difference between a ristorante and an osteria? An osteria is more informal and specializes in regional Italian food rather than national dishes.

Trattoria – This word is usually confused with osteria, but they are completely different. The Trattoria is a place even more informal than the osteria, where the cuisine is more traditional, and it is not so uncommon to chitchat with the cook or waiters. According to many Italians, the Trattoria is usually the right place to find Italian cuisine at its true core. Also, the prices are much cheaper than the Ristorante and osteria.

- **Stazione** – *Train Station*

There is no need for a deep explanation about this place. It is, however, interesting to notice that in Italian, the word "Stazione" works perfectly on its own, without saying what kind of station it is, as in English.

Even if there are other kinds of Stazioni in the country, such as the subway or tram, they are only located in a few large cities, so they are not as common as the Stazione in Italy. So, saying Stazione is enough to find a train to take.

- **Albergo** – *Hotel*

Although the Italian translation is the one shown above, you don't have to worry too much about it: for finding a place to stay during your holiday in Italy, you will soon find many English words for such places.

Words like "Hotel", "Hostel" (sometimes translated into Ostello), and "B&B" are extremely common in Italy. Do not forget that since tourists around the world really appreciate Italy, it is not so surprising to find so many English words in this environment.

Il Sistema Metrico (Metric System)

A last useful tip: always remember that Italy uses the metric system. For this reason, it could happen that a passer-by, while responding to your directions' request, may indicate something in meters.

An example would be:

"Sto cercando un ristorante. Può aiutarmi?"

"I'm looking for a restaurant. Can you help me?"

"Ne può trovare uno a trecento metri in quella direzione!"

"You can find it three hundred meters in that direction!"

If you are visiting Italy for a few days, there is no need to learn the exact conversion between (for example) meters and yards, but knowing that one meter equals 1,09 yards may give you a picture of how much you should walk.

Continuing the previous example:

The passer-by said 300 meters, so how many yards are they? They are 328, so a little more than the ones said in meters.

Viaggiare in Italia (Travel in Italy)

If you plan to travel around Italy, it is good to know what options are available. There could be some differences compared to your home country that are useful to know to avoid stressful situations.

La Macchina (The Car)

The car remains one of the most used vehicles in the country, and almost every family owns at least one car. Cars are so popular because of a lack of widespread public transport, especially in peripheral areas. However, it is still possible to travel, even without owning a car.

As for cars, there is not much to know: car rental agencies are the best option for any tourist, and, most of the time, are located at the Aeroporto (airport).

In case you are coming from a country where there is the left-hand traffic practice (like, for example, the United Kingdom), be reminded that Italy is a right-hand traffic country. So be careful when driving!

The legal age for driving a car in Italy is eighteen years old, and for a motorcycle, the minimum driving age is fourteen years old.

The Italian translation for the English word "Car" is "Automobile". Usually, it is way more common to say the short version "Auto". Another very common Italian word is "Macchina" that is literally translated into "Machine".

I Taxi (Taxi or Cab)

The use of taxis in Italy is quite uncommon compared to other countries in the world. If you come from a state where it is sufficient to reach out from the sidewalk to see the yellow car arrive, you may find yourself in trouble once you reach the Italian peninsula.

If you, for example, come from a country where it is enough to stick out your thumb on the street to call a taxi or cab, you too may find this quite difficult, if not impossible, once in Italy.

In Italy, taxis are considered a luxury due to their high prices. So, Italians use them very rarely for traveling. For this reason, it is not common to see them passing through the streets, as they do in other countries, such as New York, because they are usually waiting for potential customers at arrival places, such as a station or airport.

Gli Autobus (The Bus)

Opposed to taxis and their luxurious image, buses are among the most used public transport in Italy with their urban and extra-urban transport system. A ticket can be bought at one of the dealers or a vending machine, to then validate it once on the bus.

The Autobus tickets are usually sold in certain stores—most of the time in Tabaccheria (literally Tobacco Shop), Biglietteria (Ticket office) or a more uncommon ticket vending machine. You can also get your ticket from the Autobus driver, but in this case, you should have to have the exact amount of money in order to pay.

Inside the Autobus, there are several red buttons with the word "Stop" written on them to reserve your stop. The Autobus is the cheapest option to travel via; therefore, it means the vehicle may be slower or even more inefficient than other public transportation services (for example, most Italian autobuses do not have an air-conditioning system installed during summer). Autobus, however, are even used for traveling outside the city, covering long distances.

It is additionally good to remember that, in Italian, the Autobus is also called "Pullman" or more archaically: "Corriera".

I treni (Trains)

I Treni (trains) are one of the most used public transportation systems in Italy. However, they still lack many comforts, and it is not so uncommon to experience a delay, especially with regional trains that are not upgraded into newer models.

Train tickets must be bought at a ticket office or ticket vending machine at the station. The ticket must be validated before getting on the train; otherwise, you risk a penalty.

It is recommended to pay a higher price and take a non-regional Treno. As previously mentioned, due to "crumbling couches", delayed trains, and the lack of comforts, such as air-conditioning or functioning electrical sockets, it is recommended to pay more and travel on a newer Treno like the Freccia (Arrow) or Italo.

Here are some common sentences used in a travel context:

- **Dove è la biglietteria?**
Where is the ticket office?

- **Quando arriva il prossimo autobus?**
When will the next bus arrive?

- **Può chiamare un taxi?**
Can you call a taxi?

- **Vorrei noleggiare una macchina.**
I'd like to rent a car.

- **Qual è la prossima fermata?**
What is the next stop?

To sum up:

1. The automobile (car) is the most used means of transportation in Italy. Usually, it is possible to rent a car after arriving at the aeroporto (airport). The English word "car" can also be translated as "auto", a shortened and common version of automobile or "macchina".

2. Taxis are not so widely used compared to other countries due to their high prices. That is why foreign tourists use them more.

3. The autobus (bus) is the cheapest option for traveling inside or outside cities. They can be called "autobus", "bus" or "pullman".

4. Although many Italians use them, the Treni (trains) are subject to a lack of quality and delays, especially the cheapest ones.

Mangiare in Italia (Eating in Italy)

Food in Italy is one of the most important aspects of Italian tradition, along with the holidays, and there are some unwritten rules about how to behave while eating and what kind of food is acceptable.

In this chapter, you are going to see how food in Italy works and the main differences with English-speaking countries like the United Kingdom and the United States. You will also see what Italians consider wrong, or even unorthodox, about food and learn the most common and essential sentences that you need to know in this particular environment.

La Colazione (Breakfast)

It can be difficult to talk about specific meals since each person is different and their habits may change.

Overall, though, there are still some established "Colazione" (breakfast) traditions followed by many Italians. Like a meal that is made of sweet-baked food and dairy, such as:

Latte	–	Milk
Cereali	–	Cereals
Cornetto	–	Croissant

Regarding croissants, Italian gives importance to the differences between an Italian "cornetto" (the famous ice cream) and an Austrian or French croissant.

Biscotti	–	Cookies
Marmellata	–	Jam
Miele	–	Honey
Caffè	–	Coffee

Of course, with "Caffè" Italians do usually mean the classic espresso in a small cup. If the "Caffè" is with milk, it will be called a "Macchiato".

Cappuccino	–	Cappuccino
Fette biscottate	–	Rusks

These are generally the food that can be found on a table during a traditional Italian "Colazione".

Children usually have breakfast with milk and cereals, biscuits or other baked pastry, while adults drink cappuccinos or coffee.

In particular, espresso is a fundamental part of many Italian people's routine. Most Italians drink one or more espressos during the day, especially at breakfast and after a meal.

It is common for waiters in restaurants to ask if you want a coffee at the end of your meal.

On the other hand, a savory breakfast is uncommon but not so rare among Italians. Usually, it consists of food like:

Tramezzino	–	Sandwich
Pizza	–	Pizza
Focaccia	–	Focaccia bread

It is not part of Italian culture to eat bacon and eggs in the morning, as they are considered main meals—although there are surely people who have this kind of breakfast.

The main difference between an Italian and American breakfast is the coffee: Italy's tradition does not, usually, include take-away coffee, and in bars, an espresso is a much more common drink at a table or bar counter. It is also served in a ceramic or glass little cup.

Now let's look at a couple of terms related to the "Colazione" and coffee.

Caffè macchiato – In the English language, it is often referred to as "Macchiato" (Stained). A macchiato is made by adding some drops of milk to the coffee. It can be caldo (hot) if the added milk has been previously boiled, or freddo (cold) if the milk was from the fridge.

The biggest difference between the two, apart from the temperature, is that the hot macchiato has foam on top due to the milk emulsion.

Caffellatte – Pay attention to this word: in English-speaking countries, it is common to ask for a "Latte" to get this drink, but if you are going to order a "Latte" in Italy, you will simply get a glass of milk.

Caffellatte is a long drink, the opposite of a macchiato, which involves adding some coffee to a cup of milk.

Il Pranzo e la Cena in Italia (The Lunch and the Dinner in Italy)

Lunch is often considered the most important meal in Italian culture. Although a hectic life has led to more and more people spending less time at the table, the tradition of gathering around the table during Sunday lunch remains strong among Italian people.

Lunch is also the most elaborate meal and is divided into several courses (Christmas and Easter traditional meals revolve around lunch).

But how is an Italian meal composed?

Antipasto – Antipasto (Appetizer) means "before the meal" and is the first course served at the table. Within time, the antipasto gained a higher value in Italian cuisine, and for this reason, it is generally offered only during special events (such as Christmas) or for lunch at a restaurant.

The appetizer can be presented in two different forms: Antipasto di terra (translated as "land-food appetizer"), which is usually composed of salami, cheese, and croutons; and the Antipasto di mare (translated as "seafood appetizer"), which is mainly fish and shellfish. Usually, the chosen kind of appetizer varies according to the daily menu, in order to follow the same concept of the next dishes.

Primo – Primo means "First", is the main course of the meal, and is usually composed of pasta, minestra, and soups. In the Mediterranean diet, pasta is an important meal, which often takes the place of the next dish since it is a high-carbohydrate meal.

Each type of pasta has its specific name and is divided into long, short, and small pasta (the latter is used for minestra).

The English word "soup" is also different in Italian culture. It can be divided into three different dishes:

> - Minestra – Obtained from cooked and blended vegetables or legumes. It can be served with or without pasta.
> - Brodo – A hot and savory liquid made by boiling different types of meat (from beef to chicken) with tortellini, a ring-shaped pasta stuffed with meat and Parmigiano cheese. Brodo can also be translated into "Broth".
> - Zuppa – A thick liquid made of fish or vegetables, usually combined with stale bread softened by the cooked soup. The word zuppa is translated into "soup", but it literally means "soaked".

These dishes are usually flavored with some grated cheese. The most loved cheese is the Parmigiano Reggiano, but other types of cheese made of cow's milk (or even sheep's milk like the Pecorino) are also used and these change depending on the Italian region and personal taste.

Secondo – The third course of the Italian meal is the "Secondo" (Second). This category includes more or less all the other dishes that are not combined with the pasta, such as meat, vegetables, and fish cooked in any way.

Sometimes the "Primo" affects the "Secondo", as in the case of the Brodo: like serving the broth as a Primo course and then the meat cooked in the broth as a Secondo meal.

Contorno (Side Dish) – This is usually served with the "Secondo" and is made up of all the food that may be combined with the main course, such as vegetables like potatoes, carrots, zucchini, or salad.

Dolce (Dessert) – This is the last course served in a traditional Italian meal. Typically, it is fresh seasonal fruit, dried fruit like nuts, almonds or walnuts (dried fruits are very common during the winter and Christmas season), and only occasionally desserts.

As previously mentioned, what you have seen so far is a complete Italian meal. However, some of these courses are skipped due to time, budget, or just desiring a light meal.

The dinner is usually the lighter meal of the whole Italian cuisine, especially because it comes after a rich meal like lunch and makes for better digestion in the evening. That is why many people split the "Primo" and "Secondo" respectively during lunch and dinner.

The same can be said for pizza, the most famous dish of Italian cuisine, which is usually reserved for dinner time.

Tradizioni a Confronto (Comparing Traditions)

Although the Italian menu on paper is nothing out of the ordinary, there are still some differences compared to other countries, which can lead to misunderstandings at a restaurant.

Here are some foreign traditions considered strange in Italy:

Drinking milk during lunch/dinner – In some countries, it is a habit to have lunch or dinner with a glass of milk. In Italy, the milk is not considered a regular lunch or dinner drink, so asking for a glass of milk during one of these two meals could cause confusion or even be denied—since it is not on the menu.

For Italians, milk is a beverage reserved for breakfast, and although there are circumstances where it is consumed during lunch or dinner, in these cases, the milk is considered a full meal as it is combined with other food, such as biscuits or cereals.

Pineapple on pizza – The hate towards this kind of pizza from Italians has reached its peak, so much so that it is a recurring joke. However, there is some truth behind the jokes: for many Italians, it is offensive to put pineapple on a pizza, and asking for it, if not on the menu, can cause the Pizzaiolo (the pizza maker) to complain as pizza is such an important dish of Italian cuisine and culture.

Water at a restaurant – In some countries, it is a common practice in restaurants to refill the customers' glasses with water every time they are empty. In Italy, it is not: when ordering, you will have to specify how many bottles of a certain drink you want (even water) and they will be brought to the table. Once finished, you can order again, but you will have to pay for every consumed bottle.

It is good to remember that the wine tradition in Italy is a source of pride for many of its inhabitants, which is why even if you cannot drink your milk while eating a plate of spaghetti carbonara, you can still enjoy some of the best wines in the world.

In addition to the dishes listed, there are dishes that Americans typically consider Italian, but are not.

Here are some examples:

Fettuccine Alfredo – This dish does not exist in Italian culture, and you will hardly see "Alfredo's name" appear on a menu—unless it is the name of the restaurant owner.

Spaghetti with meatballs – The famous spaghetti with meatballs that has become famous thanks to *Lady and the* Tramp is not Italian; it is an Italian-American recipe. In some Italian regions, such as Abruzzo, it is possible to find pasta dishes with meatballs, but they are very different from this American counterpart.

Spaghetti Bolognese – In Italy, there is a sauce called "Ragù alla Bolognese", which is simply composed of tomato sauce and ground beef or pork—so very different from the American version of the sauce.

On the other hand, some Italian traditions are strange in the eyes of a non-Italian:

The time spent around the table – As you saw before while learning how a traditional Italian meal is divided, the same tradition spends a very long time around the table speaking before, during, and after the meal. This happens mostly in Southern Italian regions; people will sit at the table chitchatting for hours after the meal ends.

Legal drinking age – Selling alcohol in the United States is permitted only to persons who have reached the age of 21. In Italy, the age is eighteen years old.

Ciambelle and Donuts – Although they are often compared to each other, the Italian ciambella is very different from the American donut. The ciambella has no icing; it is just a fritter pastry covered with sugar. Sometimes it can be stuffed with cream or jam, but it is more commonly empty.

Pagare al Ristorante (Pay at Restaurant)

So far, you have learned about meals both at home and at a restaurant, but as for the latter, there are still some differences that are worth discussing: paying the bill.

Some peculiarities could confuse a foreign tourist approaching this situation for the first time. Let's take a look at them:

The coperto – In Italy, when you eat at a restaurant, it is good to take into account the price of the "Coperto" (literally translated into "Covered"). The origin of this sort of "tax" is ancient and was a cost paid from customers for using an inn table.

The Coperto still appears on the Italian menu of many restaurants, and its price varies from €1 to €2 per person, including the cost of using the table (by tradition) and the waiters' services.

Tipping – Another big difference in restaurant services is the tip, or as called in Italian, "Mancia", left for the waiter who served you during the meal. In Italy, leaving a tip is rare and given only by the customer's discretion—unlike other countries where it is not only mandatory but also includes a minimum amount to pay.

Prices – In some countries, the prices are shown as net, i.e., the tax has not been added yet and is only totaled when paying the bill. In Italy, though, the menu shows full prices, so you do not have to worry about taking into account any tax later.

Common Sentences at the Restaurant (Frasi Comuni al Ristorante)

Now that you have seen how restaurants work, how meals are divided into certain courses, and the big differences between cultures, you will now see some useful sentences for this context:

1) Can I please order the...

Potrei ordinare il...

As you can see in this sentence, the conditional (that you already saw in the verbs dedicated chapters) was used and can be with any dish you want to order. You just have to be careful to use the right article.

For example:

Potrei ordinare la pasta?	Can I order the pasta, please?
Potrei ordinare il vino?	Can I order the wine, please?

The sentence turns out to be less friendly than the English counterpart, but in this case, it is enough to add a "Mi scusi" (Excuse me) at the beginning to make it more formal:

Mi scusi, potrei ordinare il vino?

2) This is delicious.

Questo è delizioso.

3) I would love some more of the…

Vorrei ancora un po' di…

This sentence turns out to be slightly more complicated than the previous ones, but it is easier to analyze it word by word:

(Io): implied subject – *I*

Vorrei: the conditional of the verb "to have" – *would love*

Ancora un po' – *some more*

Di – *of the* (it is not necessary to specify the article in Italian)

4) What is the best wine to go with this dish?

Qual è il miglior vino per accompagnare questo piatto?

5) How did you make…

Come hai preparato… (formal environment)

Come avete preparato… (towards a waiter)

Come ha preparato… (towards a cook)

6) Thank you for the delicious meal.

Grazie per il pasto delizioso.

In Italian, there is no habit of saying thank you after a meal (but you can still say it as good manners). On the contrary, Italians are used to saying a wish right before eating their meal, although it is considered bad manners according to the etiquette.

The wish is:

Buon appetito!   Enjoy your meal!

Curiously, the literal translation of this wish is "Good appetite!"

L'Italiano e i Dialetti (Italian and its Dialects)

If your purpose is to learn the Italian language, it is good to know all the hints that exist in this language. Italy is actually a very young country, considering how recently it has been united compared to other countries like the United States, and the price of this "youth" consists of different languages and traditions within Italy.

Although Italian is recognized and taught as the national language, within the country, there are dozens of different dialects, variations of the main language based on the region to which they belong.

In many cases, Italians speak a different kind of distorted Italian words, but some other Italian regions have dialects that can also be considered real languages.

One example is Sardinia: the Italian island, known throughout the world for its beautiful coasts and high-quality cheeses, has the Sardinian language. It is a truly recognized language that can sound completely different and foreign to Italians outside of Sardinia.

Although dialects are present throughout Italy, from north to south, it is in Southern Italy where you can find great influences of these linguistic variations that can often take the place of the daily spoken Italian.

For this reason, while asking for directions in Italian, people might respond with the Italian language heavily influenced by their regional dialect/s.

While this topic is not concentrated on in this book, it is still an interesting fact to take into consideration for a non-Italian speaker.

School and Study

This chapter is essential because the scholastic and working worlds are elements that influence people's lives daily.

They are also the moments in which the knowledge of Italian plays an important role in order to carry out your job at its best and follow your education as well.

In this section, you will quickly see both the Italian school and work system, and then learn a whole sequence of sentences that can be useful at any time.

Also, be reminded that you have already seen the translation of many words related to these two worlds in one of the first chapters of the guide, but do not worry: while there is a useful list to search for any word you need, in this section, you will still analyze sentences word by word.

Let's start with the Italian school system, as each country has its differences and education systems.

The School in Italy

The Italian school begins after a child's sixth birthday. Before this, the child attends asilo (kindergarten) and before that, nursery school (asilo nido). After five years of scuole elementari (elementary school), are three years of scuole medie (middle school), until scuole superiori (high school).

If elementary and middle schools are generic, high schools are divided into dozens of options based on the subject that interests the student. There are more technical and theoretical fields, but they all last an average of five years.

At about nineteen years of age, the student can enter università (university) and choose their fields of interest. Usually, university lasts three to five years.

Knowing all this is not essential, but it is important to understand the functioning of the sentences in the next examples.

To summarize:

Asilo Nido

|

Asilo

|

Scuola elementare

|

Scuola media

|

Scuola superiore

|

Università

Studying

The verb "Studiare" (to study) was mentioned in the chapter on verbs, but now it will be detailed more specifically. Although, in general, this term can indicate the act of attending a school or being a student, in reality, it is usually used to indicate the action of studying a subject (in view of an exam, for example).

In fact, although the following sentence makes sense:

Io studio all'università.

I study at the university.

It is more common to use "Frequentare" (to attend) or more directly "Andare" (to go).

They are both verbal forms used every day, and for this reason, if you use the verb "to study", nobody would think it strange, but it is important to know this difference and not be confused.

The same sentence can be said in different ways:

Io studio all'università.	–	I study at university.
Io vado all'università.	–	I go to university.
Io frequento l'università	–	I attend university.

All three make perfect sense and are used in Italian.

In the first sentence, you see:

Io – First-person singular (I)

Studio – The verb "to studiare" (study), first-person singular

All' – The preposition between A and L' (at the)

Università – Name (University)

The second sentence works in the same way, except for the verb used, while in the third sentence, it changes the preposition from ALL to L'.

To move effortlessly in the school environment, it is good to remember that in high school and university, different manners are used as well as certain sentences that make sense only in that specific context.

Italian High School

First, most students attend public schools, as the average quality of state school education is high (although with budget cuts). For this reason, there is no clear division that can be found in other countries between private and public schools.

Regarding the etiquette that is observed, there is no obligation to wear uniforms, and students are required to address the teacher (called Professore or Professoressa – Professor) with "Lei", while teachers address the student with "Tu" (You).

(Do reread the chapter dedicated to pronouns to remember the difference between "Tu" and "Lei".)

The students are called "compagni di scuola" (classmates).

Here are some terms used in the school environment:

Volontario *[Volunteer]* – This word means the student who volunteers for an oral exam with the teacher. Students often organize themselves so that there are always volunteers, and thus are not at risk of a surprise exam.

Interrogazione *[Oral exam]* – The oral exam is one of the two methods by which the student's performance is evaluated during their time in high school. The exam consists of an oral test in which the student has to answer all of the teacher's questions.

Compito *[Written test]* – Unlike the interrogation, the written test is a test in which all of the students in the class usually take part in and allows them to obtain a grade.

Speaking of grades, it is good to remember that the Italian school environment uses a grading system from 0 to 10.

Although a 0 or a 1 grade are almost impossible to get, due to their rarity (even with a failing test it is given the minimum of 2), the maximum grade one can reach is 10 (even though is usually limited to 9). The passing grade is, therefore, 6.

Giustificazione *[Excuse Note]* – "Giustificazione" can be meant in two different ways. Usually, the "Giustificazione" is an excuse note (signed by the parent/guardian or an adult student) for a school absence. This term is sometimes also used to mean a permit to skip a test, but only when it is allowed by the professor.

Here are some more useful sentences for this context:

- **Posso andare in bagno?** – Can I go to the bathroom?

Since the school system provides a sort of hierarchy, it is usual to ask first before going to the bathroom and have a permit from the teacher. The sentence can be analyzed like this:

(Io) – As usual, it is an implied pronoun – *I*

Posso – The verb "to potere" (to can), first-person – *Can*

Andare – The infinitive form of the verb "to andare" (to go) – *To go*

Al – Preposition of A + IL – *To the*

Bagno – *Bathroom*

Since there are no interrogative sentences in Italian, the English translation is:

I can to go to the bathroom?

Of course, this sentence does not make any sense in English.

- **Che voto hai preso al compito? – What grade did you get on the exam?**

This is a classic phrase said between classmates to compare their results after a test.

Let's analyze it:

(Tu) – Implied pronoun – *You*

Che – Interrogative adjective – *What*

Voto – *Grade*

Hai – The verb "to avere" (to have), second-person singular – *Have*

Preso – Past participle of the verb "to prendere" (to get) – *Got*

Al – Preposition of A + IL – *To the*

Compito – *Written test*

Even though this sentence is largely used and perfectly correct, even in spoken Italian, the first part, "Che voto", could be replaced by "Quanto" (how much), forming the sentence:

Quanto hai preso al compito? – How much did you get on the exam?

As you can see, this sentence is much preferred in spoken Italian because it is quicker and shorter to say.

- **Dove è la 5°B?** – Where is the classroom for the fifth year, section B?

As you can see from this question, there are numerous differences in the Italian version compared to the English one. First, you see the use of an ordinal number—one of its few uses in the Italian language.

In Italy, high schools divide their students into classes based on the school year (from one to five) they are attending. If the classes tend to be too crowded, they can be divided into two or more sections.

For this reason, in a school with few students, you will find only one class per school year, while in a very popular institution, there might be multiple, starting from the letter A onwards in alphabetical order.

The number refers to the year of the students in it, and the letter means the section among the various available in the school. A new student is thus assigned to a specific class and section.

Italian University

What are the main differences between a high school and a university?

First of all, let's continue to address the professor with "Lei", but now they also address the students with "Lei". Furthermore, the students among them are called "Colleghi" (Colleagues).

Speaking of differences with high school, the university grades are no longer expressed in tenths but marks out of thirty. This means that the maximum grade becomes 30, and the passing grade is 18.

Another typical concept of the university environment is the "Libretto Universitario" (University Booklet) where all the exams and grades obtained are written down by the professors. It is one of the most important documents during your time at university, so be careful.

No longer are written tests or oral exams spoken of; now, there are Esami d'appello ("Exam sessions") that take place at certain times of the year (usually September, January/March, and May/June).

The exam sessions are often reduced to the word "Appello", as you can see in this example:

- **Quando ci sarà il prossimo appello?** – When will the next exam call take place?

Let's analyze this sentence word by word:

Quando – Adverb – *When*

Ci sarà – The verb "to essere" (to be), future third-person singular – *Will be*

Il – Masculine determiner article – *The*

Prossimo – Adjective – *Next*

Appello – Noun – *Exam call*

Let's see a couple of sentences regarding daily university life:

- **C'è lezione domani?** – Will there be a lesson tomorrow?

The university system is based on a number of weekly lessons that may vary due to unexpected events or changes ordered by the professor. For this reason, it turns out to be an extremely useful and also frequent question for, and to ask, a student.

- **Dove è l'aula studio più vicina?** – Where is the nearest study room?

One of the most common aspects of Italian universities is study rooms. These are free access areas for students where they can spend time between classes or simply to study. In these areas, there is usually internet access, tables, chairs, and power sockets for a phone and/or laptop.

Common Questions and Sentences About Study

Now that you have seen the main differences between the school environments, let's look at more sentences that can be used for this reason:

- **Io studio all'Università di Lettere**

I study at the literature department

As seen before in this chapter, it is possible to use other verbs to understand the same sentence.

Verbs like:

1. *Frequentare (to attend)*
2. *Essere iscritto/a (to be enrolled)*
3. *Andare (to go)*

As a result, the interrogative form follows the same rule. The question that could be asked to those who attend university is:

- **Dove studi?** – Where do you study?

And:

- **In quale scuola vai?** – Which school do you attend?

Speaking of common questions about education, it is good to remember that these can also be placed in the past. In particular, it is common to ask what school was attended when searching for a job—in order to know if the candidate has a diploma or not.

Here are some important words to remember:

- Diploma   –   High school diploma
- Laurea   –   University Degree
- Test di ingresso   –   Entrance Test

Most Italian universities allow free student applications, and thus students can register at a specific faculty and with an immediate application to the chosen university.

However, certain universities require an entrance exam to send the application. This exam can be made as a mere criterion to reach in order to attend the university or as an exam to take to be accepted into a limited number's student university.

- Erasmus

This word is very common in the European university environment, particularly in Italy. The Erasmus is a study program that allows students who are part of it to study abroad during their educational path.

The question about the diploma can also be asked as:

- **Che scuola hai frequentato?** – Which school did you attend?

To which is important to reply, if owning a diploma:

- **Mi sono diplomato al liceo scientifico** – I graduated from the scientific high school

Let's analyze this sentence word by word:

(Io) – Implied subject – *I*

Mi – Personal pronoun – Me

Sono – First-person singular of the verb "to essere" (to be) – *Am*

Diplomato – Past participle of the verb "to diplomare" (to graduate) – *Graduated*

Al – Preposition of A + IL – *To the*

Liceo scientifico – Specific high school – *Scientific high school*

If you want to translate the sentence from Italian to English, it is:

I graduated myself at the scientific high school.

As you can see from the sentence just analyzed, "Diplomare" and "Laureare" (achieve a diploma or degree) are verbs that need a reflexive pronoun to express a certificate's achievement.

You also see how the sentence structure is slightly different from the original English counterpart. In fact, while in English a person graduates "from" a school, in Italian, a student graduates "at" a school.

It is also by directly using the verb "Avere" (to have), do you specify you own a diploma:

Io ho un diploma   I have a high school diploma

Io ho una laurea   I have a university degree

To sum up:

- Schools in Italy are divided into numerous institutions for students from the ages of three to four years up to twenty-four to twenty-five years.
- Attending a particular school can be expressed in three different verbal forms: "Studying" (to study), "Attending" (to attend), and "Going" (to go). All three forms have the same value and are freely used in spoken Italian.
- Grades in Italian high schools range from 0 to 10, with 6 being sufficient. In the university school system, however, the maximum grade is 30, and 18 is sufficient.
- To indicate that you have completed your studies, you can use the verb "Diplomare" or "Laureare" (to graduate – if high

school or university) or directly use the verb "to have" followed by the word "Diploma" or "Graduation".

Work in Italy

Just as the school environment plays an important role in life, so does work in adulthood. Thus, the two sections you will now learn are important. In particular, they are dedicated to anyone who wants to spend more time in Italy than just a holiday.

This chapter details not only everyday sentences concerning work, but also explains what working in Italy is like. Plus, you will discover some useful words to search for and keep a job in Italy.

The Word: "Lavoro"

In English, two specific terms indicate the act of working and the work itself: the verb "to work" and the noun "job". Even "work" can be used as a noun, but between the two terms, there is a slight difference since "job" makes a greater reference to a specific profession, while "work" is a generic term.

On the other hand, in Italian, there is no such difference: the term "Lavoro" means the noun, profession, and the first-person singular of the verb "Lavorare".

Here's an example:

Io **lavoro** in pizzeria.

I work in a pizzeria.

As you can see, the word "lavoro" is used as a verbal form.

Questo è il mio **lavoro**.

This is my job.

In this second example, you find the same word again, but in this particular case, it is presented as a noun, changing its meaning— although it still concerns the working environment. Obviously, there are some synonymous that can be used instead, such as "Mestiere".

Questo è il mio **mestiere**.

This is my job.

So, which is the biggest difference between "lavoro" and "mestiere"? First of all, "mestiere" cannot be used as a verb and opposite "lavoro". While there is the verb "lavorare", there is no such verb for "mestierare".

The little difference between these two Italian words can be the same as between the English words "job" and "work". If "work" represents any activity performed to obtain remuneration, the word "job" has a more specific meaning, which refers to the profession and the role someone plays in it.

Different Kinds of Jobs in Italy

This is an important topic for anyone trying to work in the *Bel Paese* (beautiful country).

In the list below, you will find terms that have been "borrowed" from English culture and are now so integrated into daily Italian language that they have been added to Italian dictionaries.

So how is work structured in Italy? First of all, you find a division based on the working week:

- Part-time

This English word joined the daily spoken Italian language many years ago. This term refers to a job with a maximum of twenty hours of weekly work divided over various days. This kind of work is often given to students or people who don't have more time to commit to longer hours of work.

- Full time

In this case, the workweek incorporates thirty-eight to forty hours divided into various days (for example, five eight-hour days).

Unlike other countries, it is good to remember that, in Italy, there is no law (at the moment) that provides for a minimum wage. Even if there are labor unions that promise to protect the worker's rights, this involves the possibility of running into job proposals with extremely low hourly wages.

Work in Italy can further be divided into two categories.

The first is the regular job, which is regulated and registered thanks to a contract signed by the two parties with established hours, the duration of the work, and, obviously, its remuneration.

On the other hand, we find the so-called "Lavoro in nero" (uncalled work) that indicates an illegal working condition in which a contract does not protect the worker and, therefore, is subject to sudden changes in schedules, duration, and pay. This type of work is also illegal due to a lack of work safety (so be very careful if you encounter this type of work in Italy!).

An additional division can be made according to the duration of the work contract.

In this particular case, there are two kinds of contracts:

- **Lavoro a tempo determinate** – Temporary Job

This kind of work contract means a short duration (usually a few months), and at its end, the contract can be renewed or annulled. This contract is very common and is usually used for testing a worker's abilities before a permanent job contract.

- **Lavoro a tempo indeterminate** – Permanent Job

This contract is the goal of many workers: with it, there is no contract end date, and thus, there is greater security and stability for the employee.

A third division of jobs is seasonal work (Lavoro stagionale): these are job positions that mainly open up in the summer (waitresses, lifeguards, guides, etc.) in response to tourism, and which are closed for autumn. For this reason, they do not give great stability to workers.

Talking At Work

The ability to communicate within a work environment is important as it is the best way to carry out your job without problems, as well as establish a good relationship with colleagues, clients, and employers.

Here are some common sentences in this environment:

"Hai controllato i tuoi turni lavorativi?"

"Have you checked your work shifts?"

As in many other parts of the world, there are many jobs in Italy where employees are asked to do certain shifts, which can change from day to day or week to week. "Il turno" (the shift) thus becomes an important aspect of the working environment.

"Puoi sostituirmi al mio turno a lavoro?"

"Can you replace me for my shift at work?"

This is a sentence you will hear more often than you would like: the willingness among colleagues to cover themselves in difficult moments. Although it can be annoying sometimes, it is what allows work to run perfectly.

"Posso avere una settimana di ferie?"

"Can I have a week off?"

Holidays are accrued while working during the year. The employees can miss work for a certain number of days and still get paid.

Talking About Work

If it is important to talk with other people during your shift, usually, our job can be a topic of conversation and common in any context as well.

Let's see how to ask and reply to questions related to work:

"Il mio lavoro è fare il cameriere."

"My job is to be a waiter."

With this sentence, you can immediately indicate your job, even if it may look too forced compared to a more natural sentence like:

"Io sono un cameriere."

"I'm a waiter."

This option flows better, yet it can be sound a bit cold, so that is why the best option is a compromise:

"Lavoro come cameriere."

"I work as a waiter."

Often during the conversation, for how long you have done the job or activity is also added so a complete sentence could be:

"Lavoro come cameriere al Bar Fragola da due anni."

"I've been working as a waiter at Bar Fragola for two years."

Let's analyze the sentence word by word:

(Io) – Implied subject, as Italian practice – *I*

Lavoro – The first-person singular present of the verb "lavorare" (to work) – *work*

Come – Adverb – *as*

Cameriere – Noun – *Waiter*

Da – Temporal preposition – *since*

Due – Number – *two*

Anni – Object – years

If, unfortunately, you are unemployed, and are looking for a job, use the sentence:

"Sto cercando lavoro come cameriere."

"I'm looking for a job as a waiter."

Or maybe you would like to look for a job in a certain environment:

"Sto cercando lavoro in centro città."

"I'm looking for a job in the city center."

If instead, you want to ask another person about their current working condition, it is obvious to ask if they are currently working. Usually, if you are not sure of the answer, it is good practice to ask only after getting into the topic:

"Stai lavorando, al momento?"

"Are you working at the moment?"

If you know that a person has a job, your question would be about the job:

"Qual è il tuo lavoro?"

"What is your job?"

Or even asking where the person is working:

"Dove lavori in questo periodo?"

"Where do you work now?"

Studying is the way to obtain a good job, and this is why so many people are getting an education in order to achieve that. Most people have a dream job, so that could be a good conversation topic.

"Che lavoro vorresti fare?"

"Which kind of job would you like to do?"

It is clear that all the sentences listed are suggestions for starting a conversation, but also to provide more words that you could insert in the dedicated section at the beginning of the book.

Usually, questions may appear that concern certain aspects of working life. One of the most classic questions is:

"Dove lavori?" – "Where do you work?"

And the reply is:

"Io lavoro in…" – "I work in…"

Then add the place where you are working. In this case, you are not talking about the company name, but rather the generic place where you work.

Here are some examples:

un ufficio	–	an office
un negozio	–	a shop
- un ristorante	–	a restaurant
- una banca	–	a bank
- una fabbrica	–	a factory
- un call center	–	a call center

Work Environment Related Words

There are several words related to the work environment, and knowing them is important to work in Italy.

Here are a couple of examples:

Curriculum

Originally a Latin word, this is an extremely common word in the working environment, and not only in Italy; it is spread all over the world. This document is a report of all previous experience, both in terms of education and work that can be fitting to obtain a certain job position.

Although it is not accepted, or even legal in other countries, in Italy, it is often asked to attach a photo to the curriculum, especially for jobs that require public interaction.

Stipendio/Busta paga – *Salary/Pay*

Of course, this also plays a fundamental role in the work environment. The salary is generally based on both hourly or monthly income. "Busta paga" is a synonym for "Salary" in most sentences.

Connected to this topic, you can find the term "Straordinari":

Straordinari – *Overtime*

Curiously, the word "Straordinari" means extraordinary and is usually used to describe people with exceptional power or with a unique talent. On the other hand, in a working environment, the word "Straordinari" means working over the usual shift to gain a higher income.

Pensione – *Retirement*

This word indicates the period of life at the end of one's working years, where you are going to obtain a monthly income thanks to the contributions paid during your working years.

Disoccupato/a – *Unemployed*

This is a condition in which a person does not work.

Licenziare – *To fire*

As you may have understood from the translation above, this is the verb most feared by every worker and indicates when someone is removed from their employment.

HACCP

In Italy, in many jobs, it is necessary to obtain this particular certificate (HACCP – Hazard Analysis and Critical Control Points) to work.

Some jobs involve contact with (or simply the presence of) food. There are different levels, and once the certificate is obtained, it is possible to work in the specific sector.

To sum up:

- The word "lavoro" can refer to the verb "lavorare" (to work) or the noun "lavoro" (job) itself. As for the noun, there is an alternative found in the word "mestiere" (job), but it cannot be used as a verbal form.

- Jobs in Italy are divided into different categories: part-time and full-time. These are also based on shifts of twenty and forty weekly hours.

- If the type of work is divided according to the contract's length, you have the "lavoro a tempo determinato" (temporary job) and the "lavoro a tempo indeterminato" (permanent job).

Relationships in Italy

How can we interact with our loved ones? What are the most common sentences used among people who love each other? And which terms are important to know in this context?

Throughout this chapter, you will find out how relationships work in Italy, firstly, by starting with one of the most important and commonly used sentences in the world...

I Love You

It is significant to focus on this expression because, in the Italian language, it is used in a specific context only; while in English, it has a much wider use. In English, "I love you" can be said to a partner or a friend, as it can mean both romantic love and friendship.

On the contrary, in Italian, there are two different sentences for expressing the different sentiments:

"Io ti amo" – "I love you"

"Io ti voglio bene" – "I love you"

As previously mentioned, in English, the sentence can have the same meaning, while in Italian, they are used in certain and different contexts.

In fact, "Ti amo" is a sentence generally used only concerning a person you are romantically involved with. A partner, girlfriend, husband—overall, the expression "Ti amo" is used towards anyone, no matter their gender since it does not change while addressing a female or male.

Whereas "Ti voglio bene" indicates a more general love, which is not necessarily a romantic one. So, although couples can also use it, this expression is used for friends and family as well.

But be careful: the verb "Amare" (to love), used in the first sentence, can be said to any person you are attached to; only the expression "Ti amo" is reserved for a romantic partner.

Now you are going to see the verb's conjugation, and then some sentences in which the verb "Amare" is given to any other person you are not romantically attached to.

Here is the present form of "Amare":

Io amo   I love

Tu ami   You love

Lui ama   He loves

Lei ama   She loves

Noi amiamo   We love

Voi amate   You love

Loro amano   They love

After seeing the conjugation, let's see some sentences:

• **"Io ti amo"**   –   "I love you"

As mentioned, overall, this sentence is reserved for a partner; however, it does not mean that it cannot be used towards friends or family, but it may sound too strong and even strange in these contexts.

In these cases, it is much better to use the alternative, "Volere".

How is this verb built? This is the verb "volere" (to want) followed by the word "bene" (good).

For example:

"Ti voglio bene."

Can be literally translated into:

"I want you good."

And, obviously, it does not make any sense since (as seen before) the correct translation is "I love you."

Anyway, the verb "Amare" can be used in other contexts too:

- **"Lui ama suo padre"** – "He loves his father"

Although it has been said that "I love you" is usually reserved only for a romantic interest, the verb "Amare" can also be used in other contexts. In this particular case, it makes sense to use this verb.

To better understand this concept, let's take a clearer example: in the following two sentences, Marco will say (in one) to his mother that he loves her. Then (in two) he will tell someone else that he loves his mother:

Marco (verso la madre): "Io ti voglio bene."

Marco (towards his mother): "I love you."

Marco (verso l'amico, parlando della madre): "Io amo mia madre."

Marco (to his friend, speaking of his mother): "I love my mother."

As you can see, in the first case, the word "voler bene" is used, while in the second, it is still acceptable to use the verb "Amare".

However, what is said in this part of the guide it is not a strict rule. It is not like if a person said "Ti amo" towards their father they would get arrested. But in daily spoken Italian language, it can sound odd since another word is used for that.

The same happens when talking with friends.

Other Words to Express "Amore"

Just like in other languages, even in Italian, there are other words used as alternatives for meaning love:

Sono pazzo di te – *I'm crazy about you*

As with the English word, even in Italian "Pazzo" means crazy. This sentence indicates a feeling of very strong love toward someone, but beware: there are two other words to indicate an erratic behavior, such as "Folle" and "Matto", but they cannot usually replace "Pazzo" in a sentence involving love. Although, in Italy, there is a popular love song called "Cuore Matto" (roughly translated as "Mad Heart").

So, adding the word "Pazzo" make the sentence's meaning a lot stronger:

Sono pazzo di gelosia. – I'm mad jealous.

This indicates a strong jealousy. However, if the word "pazzo" is not followed by any kind of sentiment towards someone, like in the first sentence, it just means a feeling.

Sono cotto di te – I'm cooked of you (literal) – I have fallen for you (meaning)

It is obvious how the literal translation does not make any sense at all. The meaning is similar to the previous sentence, although "Essere cotto" (I have fallen for you) indicates the first stage of love—when you are starting to feel interested in someone.

The word "Cotta" (that has been used as a verb in a previous sentence) can be translated into English with "Crush".

Basically, you can express the same concept with a sentence like:

Ho una cotta per te – I have a crush on you

As you can see, in this case, the literal translation turns out to be the correct one, and there are very few differences between the Italian and the English versions.

Although, in English, there are even two different words for expressing the same concept, the Italian word remains the same.

In the Italian one, you do not find the subject (I) because, as you already learned, it is implied. Another difference is the preposition used in the second to last word. English uses the word "On" that can be translated into "Su" in Italian. While, in Italian, the preposition used is "Per", which is translated into "For".

Another difference between English and Italian culture is the importance hidden behind the phrase "Ti amo" – I love you. Although how much weight this sentence has and what is the right moment to say it in a relationship is an extremely personal and subjective element (and therefore it is not possible to draw up a general rule). Generally, in Italy, it has much less importance than its American counterpart.

Though its meaning and the right moment to say it in a relationship are both personal matters (and it is not possible to make up a general rule about it), usually, in Italy, the words have less importance than in many other English-speaking countries, like the United States.

It is very common to see how important this aspect is in movies and TV Series, while in Italy, it is just a natural consequence of a strong love relationship between two people.

The Engagement in Italy

Another big difference between English and Italian cultures is based on the engagement party. When two people's relationship goes to the next step, it is common, in the United States, to hold an engagement party to announce the engagement to others and celebrate it.

This tradition in Italy, however, it is not so common; it is almost non-existent because couples would rather celebrate their relationship with marriage.

However, the word "Fidanzarsi" (to get engaged) exists in Italy, even if its initial meaning, which was very similar to the English one, has fallen into disuse. Nowadays it simply indicates two people with a romantic relationship, but without being promised to each other or with the need for an engagement ring.

The Marriage in Italy

Italian culture has changed radically through the centuries and even if it is a now a laic country, it is still difficult for many people to forget its Christian's roots. Although marriage is a legal act that recognizes the couple as such, most of the first marriages are celebrated inside churches (especially the ones from the spouses' town) and followed by a rich and very feast-like wedding lunch.

Despite this, marriages that distance themselves from Christian ones (especially marriages after a divorce and not accepted by the Church) became established in Italian culture. For this reason, they are not held in churches but other places, like a town hall.

In the Italian tradition, the bride and groom exchange the "Fede" (Wedding Ring), which is traditionally made of gold of different colors and silver, rather than diamond and other gemstones rings.

Curiously, the word "Fede" both means the wedding ring and the word "faith", highlighting the Christian origin of marriage in the country.

Throwing rice at the just married couple while they are leaving the church after the ceremony is also common and brings good luck to the couple.

Over time, the married couple will celebrate the "wedding anniversary" based on the day they were married. The "wedding anniversary" classification has an ancient origin, dating back to the Ancient Romans and is common around the world, and, of course, in Italy.

This sort of ranking starts from a minimum of one year to a maximum of 75 years, and the most important (and celebrated) in Italy are:

25 anni – Nozze d'argento	*25 years – Silver Wedding*
50 anni – Nozze d'oro	*50 years – Gold Wedding*
60 anni – Nozze di diamante	*60 years – Diamond Wedding*
75 anni – Nozze di Platino	*75 years – Platinum Wedding*

With the increase of divorces and marriages celebrated by people of an older age compared to the past (once people used to get married at only eighteen), these kinds of anniversaries are becoming more and more rare.

To sum up:

- "I love you" is usually translated into two different sentences: "Ti amo" when it is said to a romantic interest, and "Ti voglio bene" when it is said to friends or relatives.

- Despite this, the verb "Amare" can be used indiscriminately towards anyone. For example: "Amo i miei amici." – ("I love my friends.").

- Other words can express the feelings of romantic love, such as "Sono pazzo di te." ("I am crazy about you.") and "Sono cotto di te." ("I have a crush on you.").

- The engagement, in Italy, is not celebrated as much as in other countries, and although the word "Fidanzarsi" lost its initial meaning (translated as "being engaged"), in the current Italian language, it is just used for people in a love relationship.

- In Italy, marriage still has a very important role among many people and tradition, especially for its Christian origin. It is quite common also to celebrate the wedding anniversary through the years and assign a symbolic material to certain years of marriage.

Le Feste Italiane (The Italian Holidays)

For those planning a trip to Italy as tourists or who even want to live in Italy, holidays affect many aspects of life like work, school, and people's interactions. Specifically, there are many religious, non-religious, ancient, or quite new holidays that it is good to know in order not to disrespect the Italian culture and integrate into the country.

Dicembre 8 (December 8)

Christmas is the most famous holiday in the world. It is celebrated in many countries, and with a different meaning: some religiously celebrate Christmas, others treat it as a romantic holiday (like in Japan), and others still see Christmas as a more commercial activity.

In Italy, Christmas is both commercial and religious. For now, let's look at the latter.

Since Christmas in Italy mainly celebrates the birth of Jesus Christ, December 8 is dedicated to the immaculate conception that revolves around the Virgin Mary. Traditionally, it is the day for starting to decorate the Christmas tree and setting up the "Presepe".

The "Presepe" is an exhibition of objects that recreate the nativity scene; it can be minimal with just the figures of Joseph, the Virgin Mary, and Jesus in the stable, or more complex with also the city of Bethlehem. While the Christmas tree is very common among people, the Presepe is slowly falling in disuse due to its strong Christian roots. Despite this, it is often a live exhibition, with actors and real animals, of the nativity scene and is called "Presepe vivente" (live nativity scene).

This kind of holiday does not have specific wishing, although it is impossible to hear:

"Buona festa della Madonna." – "Happy Madonna's holiday."

On December 8, usually, students and workers have the day off.

Natale e Santo Stefano (Christmas and Saint Stephan)

This chapter section lists the typical customs that most Italian families practice during a holiday. Of course, every person is different, so everyone has their own point of view about holidays and way to celebrate them. This is going to be a whole picture of the Italian culture and thus is easy to understand.

Christmas eve is celebrated on December 24. Overall, it is not considered a real holiday, so many people work on this day. Italians are more used to starting the celebrations during the evening with the "Cenone" (translated as "Big dinner").

According to its Christian origins, Christmas eve is the period spent waiting for Jesus' birth, accompanied by a fish dinner. This tradition has influenced Italian society so much that even restaurants have, usually, only fish menus on Christmas eve. After dinner, Italian people are split about the traditions: some wait until midnight to exchange gifts and wishes, while others postpone the celebration to the next day.

Then, December 25 comes and Christmas! It is an established Christian tradition to attend the celebration in the city or town's church on Christmas morning. However, it is also common to see the religious function commemorated by the Pope himself on the TV.

Curiously, despite Italy's religious significance, more and more people are leaving their religion, although most Italian people still take part in the Christmas morning liturgy as per tradition. The Mass is usually followed by Christmas lunch, a hearty meal with the family. In fact, it is common to say:

Natale con i tuoi; Pasqua con chi vuoi – Christmas with your family; Easter with whomever you want

Which other sentences can come in handy in this situation? And what kind of sentences are better to wish a merry Christmas to people around you? Usually, there are two wishes:

"Buon natale!"　　– "Merry Christmas!"

"Auguri!"　　– "Best wishes!"

While the first one is a wish that can only be used at Christmas, "Auguri" is largely used for every holiday and festivity, from birthday to Easter, and kept its meaning. Basically, it is a generic wish, while "Buon Natale" is just for Christmas.

Speaking of Christmas, there is another important figure of this holiday. If morning mass represents the Christian's soul of the holiday, Santa Claus represents the most commercial one:

Babbo Natale – *Santa Claus*

The name is made of the word Babbo (Dad) and Natale (Christmas). The English translation is, thus, "Father Christmas".

Once Christmas is over, it is **December 26** or **Santo Stefano** (Saint Stephen). This day is still considered a holiday, although it does not have any particular meaning compared to the UK and the Commonwealth countries' Boxing Day. Santo Stefano is another chance to eat together with family, and, typically, the lunch consists of leftovers from Christmas lunch.

Ultimo Dell'anno e Capodanno (New Year's Eve and New Year)

The last day of the year and the first day of the next year are both celebrated around the world, but how are they celebrated according to the Italian tradition?

Usually, the Last of the Year (last day of the year) is spent at someone's will—given that there is no moral rule that requires them to spend it with family. This is why many groups of friends organize booking houses and getaways for the night.

Unlike the other holidays, December 31 is not a national holiday, so it is a working day—although there is no school as most schools close a few days before Christmas and reopen on January 7.

Tradition has it that you should wait for the "last of the year" with dinner and, just like in the case of Christmas Eve, has a typical dish to serve: the "zampone" with lentils. It is coarsely chopped pork spiced and inserted into the paw of the same animal. This dish, accompanied by lentils, is said to bring good luck.

At this point, the end of the year is expected, with the classic countdown to the fireworks and "Spumante" (sparkling wine).

The phrase in this case (apart from the classic "Auguri", which always goes well) is:

"Buon anno nuovo!"   –   "Happy new year!"

Usually, this sentence can be shortened to:

"Buon anno!"   –   "Happy (new) year!"

These kinds of wishes are often exchanged with handshakes, hugs, and kisses based on the relationship between people.

As in many other countries, there are traditions and superstitions associated with this holiday even in Italy, among which can be mentioned:

I buoni propositi del nuovo anno – The new year's resolutions

Even if it is disappearing with time, the habit of making a good intentions list with the purpose of motivating yourself for a better year than the previous one is still quite common among Italian people—although it is also very common to forget these good intentions, too, so much that it is mocked by many.

Another superstition based on the "year's end" is how an action done on this day will be repeated for the whole next year. For example, it is common to think that if a person falls on New Year's Eve, then they will keep falling throughout the new year.

Finally, let's look at the traditional holiday Italian food. As mentioned regarding the "Zampone", most Italian culture revolves around meals. Every part of the holiday is combined with a typical dish and dessert, usually only eaten during this specific period of the year.

What are the most common new year's eve and new year desserts? They are typically the same, eaten during Christmas, and the most common ones are two desserts that split Italian people's tastes.

First, is the Pandoro, a tall soft cake decorated with icing sugar. Second, is the Panettone, a sort of sweet bread loaf containing raisins, candied fruit, or even chocolate. They are both originally made in the north of Italy.

Italy does not have a typical hot beverage, such as eggnog (zabaione in Italian), like in English-speaking countries, but it is very common to drink hot chocolate during the winter season and sparkling wine on Christmas and New Year's Eve.

Epifania e la Befana (Epiphany and the Befana)

On January 6, the second holiday of the year arrives, which has a double meaning: it is both religious and commercial.

From an exclusively Christian's point of view, the "Epifania" (Epiphany) is the manifestation of Christ's divine powers. However, this holiday is mainly known as the "Befana" (Hag), which is celebrated on the same day. This holiday is aimed at children and involves giving them a large sock from the Befana. The contents of this sock may change depending on the child's behavior: if they were good, the sock is filled with various kind of sweets; if they were bad, the sock is filled with coal.

The Befana is depicted as an old witch wearing shredded clothes riding a broom. It is clear that she is strongly inspired by Santa Claus (as he appears once a year bringing gifts to good children and coal to bad children).

This holiday is only compared to Christmas since it is well-established in Italian culture by centuries. The Befana can also be found in a common nursery rhyme:

La Befana vien di notte

con le scarpe tutte rotte

con le toppe alla sottana:

Viva, viva la Befana!

La Befana comes at night

With completely broken shoes

with the patches on the skirt:

Long live the Befana!

Related to the Epiphany, another well-known saying is:

L'Epifania tutte le feste si porta via – *The Epiphany takes all the holidays away*

Naturally, this saying refers to the fact that the Epiphany is the last of a long series of holidays starting from December 8, so it works as an end to all the festivities. There aren't any particular wishes during this holiday, so it is okay just to use "Best wishes". However, you do occasionally hear, "Buona Befana!" (translated as "Good Hag!").

Carnevale (Carnival)

"Carnevale" (Carnival) traditionally begins with the Epiphany's conclusion and ends on the Tuesday before the "Mercoledì delle ceneri" (Ash Wednesday), which is the Wednesday preceding Easter. This holiday does not have any public days and, usually, it is just a way to let children dress up as books, comics, movies characters, or even with traditional masks.

Carnevale and its masks are different from region to region, with the masks based on fictional characters. The most famous ones are Pulcinella (Neapolitan mask) and Arlecchino (Venetian mask).

A popular thought was that the Carnevale's loud noises, colors, and music were needed to banish the darkness and the cold of winter, to pave the way for spring.

During these celebrations, carnival floats are commonly seen passing along Italian streets. Usually, the carnival floats look satirical, even irreverent, or are a true piece of art. Also, it is common, especially among children, to dress up as fictional characters and throw confetti in the streets.

As mentioned, Carnevale is strongly influenced by the region it is celebrated in, even the typical sweets and desserts may vary from region to region, but typically, the most famous Carnevale's sweets are the Chiacchiere (Chit-chat), a sweet pastry fritter covered with icing sugar and perfect for getting the right amount of energy to celebrate Carnevale during the cold season.

Carnival does not have any specific wishes.

Pasqua e Pasquetta (Easter and Easter Monday)

Right after Carnevale, is Pasqua (Easter) that does not have a specific day for being celebrated. Technically speaking, Pasqua is celebrated on the first Sunday after the first spring full moon, but luckily, there is no need to be an astronomer to know when Easter will be celebrated: just take a look at the calendar.

Pasqua is a public holiday, which means students and some workers have several days off. Its origins lie in Christianity, although Pasqua now has a more commercial purpose.

From a purely Christian point of view, Pasqua celebrates the resurrection of Christ and the next day, Pasquetta (Easter Monday), is called "Lunedì dell'angelo" (Angel Monday) and celebrates the meeting between the angel and the women at Jesus' tomb. Traditionally, Pasqua is celebrated with different religious rites more or less followed by the Italian population. Sunday is generally spent at home with family, while the next day is dedicated to picnics, excursions, and outdoor activities.

On the other hand, the more commercial soul of this holiday, just as with Babbo Natale and Befana, involves giving presents, usually to younger family members. In this case, the most common Pasqua gift are big eggs made of different types of chocolate, which contain surprises like toys or jewelry.

Originally, the eggs were just painted regular eggs that symbolized rebirth, but through time, this tradition evolved into the exchange of chocolate eggs and is celebrated by almost everyone in Italy.

Compared to other countries, in Italy, there is no tradition of "looking for eggs" nor the concept of the "Easter Bunny"—although it is common to give rabbits made of chocolate as a gift, even though they just represent fertility and rebirth.

In this case, it is possible to wish:

Buona Pasqua! – *Happy Easter!*

Or just:

"Auguri!" – *Best wishes!*

Concerning the traditional Italian cuisine during Easter, there is the habit of eating lamb on Sunday, which originates from the Christian side of the holiday and the redeeming nature of the animal according to Christianity. As for the desserts, besides the chocolate eggs and rabbits, it is common to eat the "Colomba" (Dove), an iced-sugar baked cake with almonds made into the shape of the bird.

Both Easter and Easter Monday are national holidays in Italy.

Festa Della Donna (Women's Day)

The Festa Della Donna (International Women's Day) is celebrated on **March 8** in honor of the social conquests achieved by women over the years. In Italy, it is common practice for men to give mimosa flowers to women they are attached to (like family members or love interests), but also as a polite gesture to female colleagues and classmates.

Obviously, in this case, the wishes are only reserved for women:

"Buona Festa Della Donna." – "Happy Woman's Day."

During this holiday, it is quite common to organize women-only dinners, and even restaurants, bars, and nightclubs have special promotions for women.

However, it is not recognized as a public holiday.

Festa Del Papà (Father's Day)

March 19 is Festa Del Papà (Father's Day), which celebrates fathers. Children usually give presents to their fathers on this day.

It is important to note that this day changes from country to country. Italy shares this date with countries like Spain, Bolivia, and a handful of other countries, while the Festa Del Papà's date changes into the third Sunday of June in other countries.

Festa Della Liberazione (Liberation Day)

This is the first Italian historical celebration and takes place on April 2, the day when Italy celebrates the liberation's anniversary from the fascist regime and Nazi occupation. It is recognized as a national holiday during which schools are closed and, usually, people do not work.

No special wishes or traditions are considered since it is a fairly recent celebration, and overall, it is a holiday that is meant to be spent doing outdoor activities, such as picnics.

Festa Dei Lavoratori (Workers' Day)

As in other countries of the world, May 1 in Italy is Festa dei Lavoratori (Workers' day). It is celebrated to honor workers' rights and to remember the sacrifices made in order to obtain them. It is recognized as a public holiday, so schools are closed and, obviously, workers have the day off.

Festa Della Mamma (Mother's Day)

The Festa Della Mamma (Mother's Day) is celebrated on **May 10**. Although it is not recognized as a public holiday, on this day, it is customary to celebrate every mother and give them gifts.

Sometimes the celebration is also extended to grandmothers.

Festa Della Repubblica (Republic Day)

On **June 2,** Italy celebrates the Festa Della Repubblica (Republic Day) in honor of the referendum held on the same day in 1946. On that date, Italian people went to vote on still being under a monarchy or becoming a republic. With 54 percent of the votes, Italy became a republic, and for this reason, June 2 is recognized as a public holiday by the state.

There are not any particular wishes for this holiday.

Ferragosto

Ferragosto is celebrated on **August 15**. It is a holiday of ancient origin, since Ancient Rome, made for giving a day of rest from the scorching summer period. It is recognized as a public holiday and traditionally celebrated by eating outdoors, hiking, going to the beach, or doing any other outdoor activities.

Curiously, Italians used to wish "Buon Ferragosto" (Happy August 15) rather than wishing "Auguri" (Best wishes) because it is not a real celebration—but more an opportunity to enjoy some rest, especially a day off from work, during summer.

Halloween

As in other countries, especially the English-speaking ones, Halloween is celebrated in Italy on **October 31.** Although this holiday became popular thanks to movies and television, it still a fairly new celebration in Italian culture.

It is still not a habit for Italian children to do "trick-or-treat" in the streets to get sweets, but it is seen as an occasion to dress up children as fictional characters like during Carnevale (Carnival).

On the other hand, radical Christians in Italy are strongly against this holiday since it is seen as blasphemous.

Halloween is not a public holiday.

Ognissanti e Commemorazione Dei Morti (All Saints' Day/All Souls' Day)

"Ognissanti", or also called "Tutti i Santi", (All Saints), is a Christian holiday on **November 1** in which all the saints are celebrated, even those not canonized. It is recognized as a public holiday, so a day off school and, usually, work. There is not a specific tradition to follow, except for Christian's processions towards the cemeteries to bless the tombs.

The "Commemorazione dei Morti" (All Souls' Day), or more commonly called "Giorno dei Morti", (Day of the Dead), is celebrated the following day, on **November 2**. Although this is not a public holiday like Ognissanti, on this day, many people honor the dead by visiting cemeteries and bringing them flowers.

In both cases, there are no particular wishes.

Santi e Patroni in Italia (Saints and Patron Saints in Italy)

Given the strong Christian traditions in Italy's past, you may have noticed that Santi (Saints) are very important. Every Italian town and city has a Santo Patrono (Patron Saint) to represent them, and on the day that Santo Patrono is celebrated, it is considered a public holiday, so schools and some stores are closed.

The cultural importance of Santi Patroni and Santi-related celebrations change from place to place and region to region. For example, in Southern Italy, celebrating the Santi has an important impact on the cities' traditions, and on people living in the cities, much more than in other parts of Italy.

Proverbi (Proverbs)

In the previous chapter, many Italian figures of speech were detailed. Given that Italy is a multicultural peninsula, thanks to its many regions, the figures of speech also vary from area to area.

In this chapter, proverbs, the other side of the coin, will be discussed. The well-known proverbs have popular origins and are rooted over time. They stem from oral tradition and convey a teaching so that other people can learn from it.

Proverbs of this type are a powerful tool in the hands of those who want to learn the Italian language: it is much easier to learn words when the message they transmit is interesting. For this reason, the original proverb is offered, then its translation and meaning. A good way to remember these proverbs is to try to associate the English equivalent with the Italian proverb.

Modi Di Dire e Frasi Fatte (Common Sayings and Set Phrases)

This section is quite long, but you don't need to learn it all at once. Just like the dedicated words chapter, the main purpose is to give you a point of reference for all the dialects and phrases that cannot be translated literally. Just think about the common saying: "Like shooting fish in a barrel." If you tried to translate it into Italian, it would make no sense. However, if you learn the meaning of a certain common saying instead, then it will be easier to recognize, and you can use it in spoken Italian too.

Why are common sayings so important?

1. If you do not know them, you will not understand a sentence's meaning.

2. If you use a common saying, the impression you give of your mastery of Italian will improve drastically.

Of course, it is impossible to list all the Italian ways without making thousands of chapters out of them, so only the most popular and used ones are listed.

Let's start:

Abbaiare alla luna (*to bark at the moon*). Useless complaints because we are not heard or the person we are talking to do not have any interest in hearing us; just like a dog that barks at the moon.

Abbassare la cresta *(to lower the crest)*. Don't be too cocky; be humbler instead. In fact, the crest stated in the common saying is the same as a chicken.

Abboccare all'amo *(to bite the hook)*. Fall into a trap or provocation.

Andare a braccetto (*go hand in hand*). *Get along.*

Andare a letto con i polli (*go to bed with the chickens*). Going to bed early. This common saying takes its origin from an old tradition that keeps going on in Italy even nowadays. Chickens have the habit of retreating into the henhouse as soon as the sun goes down and wake up at dawn. This is why the farmers used to go to bed very early (as the chickens do) and woke up just as early.

Andare a tentoni (*to go while groping*). Not having clear ideas. The common saying represents the act of stretching out the arms and touching things while in the dark because it is impossible to see.

Andare a vuoto (*to go empty*). Cannot do it; failing; do not succeed.

Andare a zonzo (*to go for a stroll*). Walking aimlessly, just for fun or for passing the time.

Andare in bestia (*to become a beast*). Raging over something like a beast; losing self-control; getting angry; becoming violent.

Andare in bianco (*to go in white*). Another common saying for failure.

Andare in vacca (*to go in cow*). Getting into bad conditions or ruining everything.

Arrampicarsi sugli specchi (*to climb the mirrors*). Making useless attempts or working hard for nothing in an already useless challenge.

Aspettare al varco (*to wait at the gate*). Waiting for someone while hiding; also be ready to face them as soon as they are near.

Attaccare bottone (*to stick a button*). Starting a conversation with someone.

Avere la coda di paglia (*to have a tail made of straw*). Feeling judged and attacked for doing something wrong.

Avere una fifa blu (*to have a blue fear*). Having a great fear of something. Curiously, the word "blue" (blu) states sadness in the English language, while in Italian, it states fear.

Avere fegato (*to have liver*). Being brave. The common saying's origins are from the Greek myth of Prometheus, the titan who took the fire from the gods to give it to human beings. Because of that, Prometheus was bound to a rock, and his liver was eaten every day by an eagle. Then, the liver would grow back in order to be eaten the next day again.

Avere culo (*to have butt*). Being lucky.

Avere gli occhi foderati di prosciutto (*to have the eyes covered by ham*). Don't see the evidence.

Avere il pollice verde (*to have the green thumb*). Being extremely gifted at taking care of plants and flowers.

Avere la luna storta (*to have the crooked moon*). Being moody, unreasonably irritable, and ready to fight. A little trivia: the character Remus Lupin from the fantasy saga *Harry Potter* is also called "Moony", while in the Italian version of the books, he is called "Lunastorta".

Avere la pelle d'oca (*Goose bumps*). Shiver in cold or fear. In the English language, there is a variation of this common saying involving another animal than the goose: having chicken skin.

Battere il ferro finché è caldo (*to beat the iron while it's still hot*). Knowing how to take advantage of good opportunities and start something when the situation is favorable.

Battere la fiacca (*to beat the weariness*). Being unenthusiastic and lazy.

Bruciare le tappe (*to burn the stages*). Proceed at a fast pace, quickly overcoming obstacles, and having no hesitation.

Cadere dalla padella nella brace (*fall from the pan to the grill*). Worsening a situation; finding an alleged remedy that, instead, soon turns out to be worse than the problem.

Calzare a pennello (*wear as a brush*). Wearing something perfectly; being the perfect size.

Cercare il pelo nell'uovo (*to search the hair in the egg*). Being picky.

Cercare rogne (*to look for trouble*). Looking purposely for difficult and risky situations.

Cercare un ago in un pagliaio (*look for a needle in a haystack*). Sentence used to indicate a desperate and impossible challenge.

Chiudere un occhio (*to close one eye*). Pretending not to know something.

Cogliere con le mani nel sacco (*to catch someone with his hands in the bag*). Surprise someone in the act.

Conoscere i propri polli (*to know your chickens*). Knowing well the people you are involved with.

Contare quanto il due di briscola (*to have the same value as the two in the game Briscola*). Do not be relevant. This common saying came from the popular Italian card game, Briscola, in which the ace is the card of maximum value while the two is worth nothing (so much that it is always discarded while playing with three other players)

Dar del filo da torcere (*giving some thread to twist*). Make something, usually a challenge, difficult to others to not be defeated yet.

Dare i numeri (*giving numbers*). Looking crazy; saying and doing something incoherent; talk nonsense.

Dare il benservito (*pink slip*). Throw someone out; fire someone from work; abandon someone.

Dare un colpo al cerchio e uno alla botte (*hit both the circle and the barrel*). Distribute appropriately praise or blame, reasons or wrongs, in order not to displease anyone; carry on two deals, taking care of them alternately; try to juggle without displeasing anyone; do not take a clear position.

Darsi la zappa sui piedi (*hit ourselves with the hoe*). To reason; to bring evidence against one's assumption; to harm oneself unintentionally.

Dormirci sopra (*sleeping on it*). Postpone a decision by sleeping on it and thinking about it with a fresher mind.

Entrare negli anta (*entering the forty*). Turn forty.

Essere al verde (*being at green*). Do not have any money or do not have something in particular anymore.

Essere baciato dalla fortuna (*being kissed by luck*). Being extremely lucky. It is based on how luck is usually depicted as a blindfolded woman. So being kissed by a woman who cannot see it is considered unique.

Essere in alto mare (*being on open sea*). Being far from a solution to a problem or something's conclusion. Just like being in a boat on the open sea, maybe during a storm.

Essere in una botte di ferro *(being in an iron barrel)*. Being in a situation of tranquility; being faultless; or, usually, just being safe.

Essere in vena *(being on vein)*. Feeling full of strength or creativity; overall, being in the best condition to do something.

Essere l'ultima ruota del carro *(being the last wheel of the cart)*. Being the least important person in a group.

Essere negato *(being hopeless)*. Being completely unsuitable; not being accepted at all (for an activity or discipline).

Essere sano come un pesce *(being as healthy as a fish)*. Having good health.

Essere un figlio di papà *(being a father's son)*. It is said of a young person who leads a comfortable life or who makes their way through economic and social position, authority, or prestige, being protected by their father.

Essere una frana *(being a landslide)*. Being unable to achieve something.

Essere una spugna *(being a sponge)*. Being a drunk; a heavy drinker.

Far buon viso a cattivo gioco *(making good faces while playing dirty)*. Getting used to the good in unpleasant situations.

Far secco *(dry someone)*. Killing someone.

Far vedere i sorci verdi *(let others see the green rats)*. Make others angry or even scaring someone and creating a series of difficulties.

Fare cilecca *(misfire)*. Missing life's goals; failing.

Fare di ogni erba un fascio *(make each bundle a bundle)*. Not knowing how to distinguish between totally different things; having strong prejudices; comparing different things.

Fare il buono e il cattivo tempo *(doing good and bad)*. Exercise power over a group of people.

Fare la cresta su qualcosa *(cresting on something)*. Increase the price of something to gain an advantage.

Fare la nanna *(doing the nanna)*. Sleeping. A common saying, especially by children.

Farla finita *(get it over with)*. Stop something immediately.

Farla franca *(doing it candid)*. Being able to get away with impunity; do an unlawful and reprehensible action without being caught.

Gettare la polvere negli occhi a qualcuno *(throwing dust into someone's eyes)*. Deceive someone.

Gettare la spugna *(throwing the sponge)*. Giving up on something.

Indorare la pillola *(gild a pill)*. Making something less bitter; mitigate displeasure with appropriate words; prettify.

Lasciarci le penne *(lost the feathers)*. Suffer serious harm or literally dying.

Leccarsi i baffi *(lick the mustaches)*. Feeling pleasure while eating something delicious.

Leccarsi le ferite *(lick the wounds)*. Seek comfort in disappointment or failure; comfort ourselves.

Legarsela al dito *(tying to the finger)*. Hold a grudge; promising revenge.

Levare le tende *(remove the tents)*. Leaving a place.

Mandare a monte *(sending to mountains)*. Let something fail; prevent the realization of something.

Mandare a quel paese *(sending to the town)*. To send someone away in a bad way; get rid of it quickly.

Mangiare la foglia *(eating the leaf)*. Understanding the situation; understanding the hidden meaning of a certain message; realizing that things are not as they look.

Metterci una pietra sopra *(put a rock over it)*. Getting definitely over something.

Mettere i bastoni tra le ruote *(put sticks through wheels)*. Get in the way.

Mettersi le mani nei capelli *(putting hands through the hair)*. Despair.

Molto fumo e poco arrosto *(much smoke and little roast)*. A lot of appearance and little substance.

Nella botte piccola ci sta il vino buono *(in the little barrel there is the finest wine)*. A common saying used to praise a person of little height that might feel inferior to those who are taller.

Non aver peli sulla lingua *(do not have hair on your tongue)*. To express oneself frankly even at the cost of being judged critical and rude.

Non cavar un ragno dal buco *(do not pull out any spiders from a hole)*. Get nothing despite the efforts; do not finish anything.

Non svegliare il can che dorme *(do not awake the sleeping dog)*. Do not tease who looks dangerous.

Pagare alla romana *(paying like a Roman)*. Dividing the paying bills or paying your part of the bill.

Parlare al vento *(speak to the wind)*. Speaking while being ignored.

Passare un brutto quarto d'ora *(spending an awful quarter of an hour)*. Being in an awful situation.

Perdere il pelo ma non il vizio *(losing the fur but not the bad habits)*. Do not believe in any people changing.

Piangere lacrime di coccodrillo *(crying crocodile tears)*. Too late to regret something.

Predicare bene e razzolare male *(preach good but rummage through badly)*. Saying always the right thing but, actually, acting in a mean and disrespectful way.

Prendere un granchio *(taking a crab)*. Misunderstanding something big.

Saperne una più del diavolo *(knowing better than the devil)*. Being very smart.

Tutto fa brodo *(anything goes)*. An unstable economic situation and using the last resources for doing something.

I Proverbi Più Famosi (The Most Famous Proverbs)

Le bugie hanno le gambe corte. – *Lies have short legs.*

Lies are discovered immediately; they have short legs and cannot go far. Curiously, the proverb that lies have a long nose is far more common. This second version comes from the spread of the novel *Pinocchio* in Italy (in Collodi).

Non è tutto oro quel che luccica. – *Not all that glitters is gold.*

Not all beautiful things are, in the end, the best. A proverb that warns of pure appearance, seeking a deeper meaning.

Anche l'occhio vuole la sua parte. – *The eye also wants its part.*

Even the outward appearance affects the judgment of things or people. Even if the outward appearance should be less important than what we have inside, it would be hypocritical to claim that it has no weight in our choices.

Morto un papa se ne fa un altro. – *When a Pope dies, another one is appointed.*

No one is irreplaceable. This proverb comes from the practice of appointing a Pope after the death of his predecessor, with the famous smoked ceremony announcing the new pontiff.

Chi sa fa e chi non sa insegna. – *Who knows how to do it, does it. And who does not know to do it, teaches.*

More and more people are teaching how to do something without having an idea of how to do it. Who can do something, does it. Whoever cannot do it, starts talking.

Lontano dagli occhi, lontano dal cuore – *Out of sight out of mind.*

Many people believe that distance strengthens love, and sometimes it is true. But often staying away also makes love dim.

Chi ha i denti non ha pane, e chi ha pane non ha i denti. – *He who has teeth has no bread, and he who has bread has no teeth.*

The only people who truly appreciate something are those who don't have it but would like to have it.

A buon intenditor, poche parole. – *Few words to the wise.*

Who can listen does not need too many words, just as those who are ready to hear do not need any cry.

Fare il passo più lungo della gamba. – *Take a step longer than the leg.*

Don't calculate the risks and costs of an action well overestimating your capabilities.

Uomo avvisato mezzo salvato. – *Forewarned is forearmed.*

Seeing a danger still gives us the chance to avoid it—if we know how to seize the opportunity.

Chi semina vento raccoglie tempesta. – *Who seeds wind shall harvest storm.*

A concept very similar to that of Karma. Who perpetuates evil deeds will be repaid with the same coin.

Vivi e lascia vivere. – *Live and let live.*

A proverb that preaches tolerance.

Il gioco è bello quando dura poco. – *The game is nice when it doesn't last long.*

Even the best things must end before they become annoying. Too much too bad, using another figure of speech.

Tra moglie e marito non mettere il dito. – *Don't put your finger between husband and wife.*

Even if the intent is positive, it is not good to interfere in a relationship between two other people.

Ne uccide più la lingua che la spada. – *The pen kills more people than the sword.*

An invitation not to underestimate the strength and consequences that certain words can have.

A caval donato non si guarda in bocca. – *Don't look a gift horse in the mouth.*

A gift must be accepted without any reservation and without evaluating its value. The proverb stems from the habit of checking the teeth of a horse before purchasing it to evaluate its health.

L'erba del vicino è sempre più verde. – *The neighbor's grass is always greener.*

It is easier to appreciate what others have rather than what we have.

Meglio soli che male accompagnati. – *Better alone than in bad company.*

It is necessary to carefully choose the people around us, as not all company is worthy of others.

Il mondo è fatto a scale. C'è chi scende e c'è chi sale. – *The world is made up of stairs. There are those who descend, and those who ascend.*

There are times when it seems that everything goes wrong, but (like a series of stairs) life offers both ascents and descents; you have just to overcome the moment.

L'amore non è bello se non è litigarello. – *Love is not good if there are no arguments*

In a good report, there is a discussion, even a heated one, between two partners.

Chi è causa del suo mal pianga sé stesso. – *Who causes his own illness will cry himself.*

When we are the cause of our misfortunes, we can only reproach ourselves. This proverb has ancient origins and is a reinterpretation of a verse of the "Divine Comedy" by Dante Alighieri.

Chi troppo e chi niente. – *There are those who have too much and those who have nothing.*

Luck is unfairly distributed.

Chi si loda si imbroda. – *Whoever praises himself gets messed up.*

Literally: "He who weaves his praise ends up in the broth." Those who praise themselves too much end up damaging themselves.

Chi dorme non piglia pesci. – *Who sleeps does not catch fish.*

The fisherman who falls asleep does not notice the fish that bites. A proverb that warns against idleness and laziness.

Dagli amici mi guardi Iddio; che dai nemici mi guardo io. – *God protect me from friends; I take care of my enemies.*

From an enemy, you know what to expect; it is the betrayal of a friend that hurts the most.

Altezza mezza bellezza. – *Being tall means already being half beautiful.*

A typical proverb said by those who are tall and want to taunt those who are shorter, who respond with:

Nella botte piccolo, c'è il vino buono. – *In the small barrel, there is good wine.*

Precisely because the smaller the barrel, in general, the more the wine is prized.

Non è bello ciò che è bello ma è bello ciò che piace. – *What is beautiful is not beautiful, but what is pleasing is beautiful.*

There is no single ideal of beauty; it is subjective. Curiously, there is a dialect variant that is known throughout the country: "Ogne scarrafone è bell 'a mamma soja", which literally means "Every cockroach is beautiful for its mother", a proverb that also indicates the infinite love of mothers.

Il riso abbonda sulla bocca degli stolti. – *Laughter abounds on the mouth of fools.*

Laughing without demeanor is a symptom of rudeness and stupidity.

Sbagliando si impara. – *You learn by making mistakes.*

We must value our mistakes because we can learn and improve from them. There is a popular (grammatically wrong) variant that is "Nessuno nasce imparato" or "No one is born learned".

Chi disprezza compra. – *He who despises buys*

Often, those who speak ill of something are actually much closer to it than one would think.

Chi si fa i fatti suoi campa cent'anni. – *Who does his business, lives for a hundred years.*

The real elixir of long life is not to pay attention to others and to live thinking of our own facts.

Occhio non vede, cuore non duole. – *Eye does not see; heart does not hurt.*

If you don't know that a fact has happened, you can't suffer from it.

Rosso di sera, bel tempo si spera. – *Red sky at night, hopefully good weather the next day.*

It is a popular belief that when the sky takes on reddish shades at sunset, the day that follows will be characterized by good weather.

Il lupo perde il pelo ma non il vizio. – *The wolf loses the hair but not the vice.*

Beware of trusting those who have shown themselves to be negative: it is difficult to really change.

Oggi a me domani a te. – *Today to me, tomorrow to you.*

Life is a wheel, and everyone has positive and negative moments.

Ogni lasciata è persa. – *Every opportunity left is lost.*

We must never postpone when we are faced with an occasion because it is not said that this will recur in the future.

L'ospite è come il pesce: dopo tre giorni puzza. – *The guest is like fish: after three days it stinks.*

Guests are more welcome if their visits don't last too long.

Can che abbaia non morde. – *Barking dog does not bite.*

Often those who show themselves to be the most violent and aggressive are actually less dangerous than ever.

La via dell'Inferno è lastricata di buone intenzioni. – *The road to Hell is paved with good intentions.*

Probably one of the most beautiful proverbs of all: mistakes are often made or wrong things done, shielding behind good intentions.

Non si può avere la botte piena e la moglie ubriaca. – *You can't have your cake and eat it too.*

You can't have everything. The literal translation means "You can't have the barrel full of wine and the wife drunk at the same time".

Tra il dire e il fare c'è di mezzo il mare. – *Between saying and doing there is the sea.*

Everyone is good at words, but only some act. There is a big difference between saying something and doing it.

Chi va con lo zoppo, impara a zoppicare. – *Who goes with the lame, learns to limp.*

It is very easy to learn from others, especially the negative aspects.

Chi si accontenta gode. – *Whoever is satisfied, enjoys it.*

Rather than always looking at what we do not have, we should enjoy what we have and be satisfied with it. There is a very famous song in Italy, "Vasco Rossi", where these words are found, even if they are later denied.

Finché c'è vita c'è speranza. – *As long as there is life, there is hope.*

We must never lose hope. This proverb has ancient origins: in Latin, there was a similar phrase, "Spes ultima dea" referring to the goddess of Hope, who remained even when all the others left the Earth.

Natale con i tuoi; Pasqua con chi vuoi. – *Christmas with your family; Easter with whomever you want.*

This was mentioned in the Italian holidays section. Christmas, by tradition, is spent with family; Easter, on the other hand, can be spent with friends and acquaintances.

Il buon giorno si vede dal mattino. – *The good day starts in the morning.*

A good start is often a good omen for everything to continue in the best way.

I soldi non fanno la felicità. – *Money does not buy happiness.*

Although wealth is a dream shared by all, money does not make us happy (as demonstrated by unhappy millionaires who live a life of extremes).

Il bue dice cornuto all'asino. – The ox says horned to the donkey.

There are those who criticize the faults of others without realizing that they have the same (and often worse) faults. In Italian, "Cornuto" is a fairly serious offense, as it means having been betrayed by your wife.

Chi troppo vuole nulla stringe. – *Who wants too much, gets nothing.*

A proverb similar to that of "Chi si accontenta gode" that once again underlines the importance of appreciating what one has.

Chi rompe paga e i cocci sono i suoi. – *Who breaks pays and the pieces are his.*

If you break an object, you have to pay for it, and at most, you can keep the broken object. This is practically an unwritten rule of many Italian shops and, in fact, the proverb is also taught to small children so that they do not break anything.

Tentar non nuoce. – *There's no harm in trying.*

Rather than doing nothing, it is always better to try.

Se non è zuppa è pan bagnato. – *If it's not soup, it's wet bread.*

This is a proverb that could confuse a person who is learning Italian for the first time, but fortunately, "zuppa" has already been mentioned. This is a soup with stale bread, which is why the proverb means: "Two things are the same even if apparently different".

Tra i due litiganti il terzo gode. – *Between two parties, the third gains.*

When two people argue, there is always a third that takes advantage of the situation.

Tutto fumo e niente arrosto. – *All smoke and no roast.*

Often referred to a person who appears to be exceptional but who turns out to be less than they seemed to be.

Fortunato al gioco, sfortunato in amore. – *Lucky at cards, unlucky in love.*

If a person proves lucky in the game (often cards), then they will be unlucky in love. Often the reverse phrase is also used and is a typical Italian belief.

Si stava meglio quando si stava peggio. – *It was better when it was worse.*

A nostalgic phrase that indicates that when everything seemed worse than today, we actually lived better. Often, in Italy, it is used to allude to old political administrations.

Al cuore non si comanda. – *You can't control your heart.*

The heart does not follow reason but one's feelings. This proverb is often used to justify an apparently impossible love.

Chi trova un amico trova un tesoro. – *Whoever finds a friend finds a treasure.*

A friend is far more precious than any other treasure. Little curiosity: there is a movie with this title of a famous couple composed by Bud Spencer and Terrence Hill.

Non svegliar il can che dorme. – *Do not awaken a sleeping dog.*

Do not provoke those who are calm and placid but potentially dangerous. There is a variable of this proverb that says: "Non c'è peggior cattivo di un buono che diventa cattivo", or "There is none so bad than a good person who becomes bad". Also, in this case, the importance of not provoking others is underlined.

Chi cerca, trova. – *Who seeks, finds.*

If you want to get something, don't just sit still. This proverb has a similar meaning to that of "He who sleeps does not catch fish".

È inutile piangere sul latte versato. – *It is useless to cry over spilled milk.*

After making a mistake, it is useless to cry and despair.

Chi tace acconsente. – *Whoever keeps silent, agrees.*

A proverb against those who do nothing but then complain. If you remain silent, you are an accomplice to what has happened.

L'abito non fa il monaco. – *The dress does not make the priest.*

It is not our appearance that tells us who we are, but what we have on the inside. Similar in meaning is "Non si giudica un libro dalla copertina", which translates as: "You don't judge a book by its cover".

Paese che vai usanza che trovi. – *Country you go, custom you find.*

Never has a proverb proved to be more suited to such a manual: each country has its customary uses. There is a second proverb with a similar meaning, "Mogli e buoi, dei paesi tuoi", which translates as: "Wives and oxen from your countries".

Chi fa da sé fa per tre. – *Those who act alone are worth three.*

Act on your own and roll up your sleeves without waiting for them to help you guarantees the best result.

Non tutte le ciambelle escono con il buco. – *Not all donuts come with a hole.*

It is not certain that everything ends as you expect.

Non tutto il male vien per nuocere. – *Not all evil comes to harm.*

Sometimes what appears to be a negative event actually conceals a benefit.

Una mela al giorno leva il medico di torno. – *An apple a day keeps the doctor away.*

One of the most famous proverbs in Italy: by eating an apple a day, thanks to its beneficial effects, you remain healthy and keep the doctor away.

Una rondine non fa primavera. – *A swallow does not make spring.*

Swallows are very present in Italy and often coincide with the arrival of spring. But a single swallow does not mean that spring has arrived.

Quando il gatto non c'è i topi ballano. – *When the cat is not there, the mice dance.*

When no one is in control, everyone does what they want.

Meglio tardi che mai. – *Better late than never.*

A proverb that is found in many other countries too: it is never late to start; it is always better than to do nothing.

Non c'è peggior sordo di chi non vuol sentire. – *There are none so deaf as those who will not hear.*

It is needless to talk to those who don't want to listen.

La gatta frettolosa fece i gattini ciechi. – *The hasty cat made the kittens blind.*

Doing things in a hurry never leads to positive results.

La fortuna aiuta gli audaci. – *Fortune favors the bold.*

Luck is more benevolent towards those who conquer it. This sentence has an ancient origin, deriving from the Latin expression of Virgil: "Fortuna audaces iuvat".

Meglio un uovo oggi che una gallina domani. – *Better an egg today than a chicken tomorrow.*

An immediate certainty is better than future uncertainty.

Chi va piano va sano e va lontano. Chi va forte va alla morte. – *Who goes slow and steady wins. Whoever goes fast goes to death.*

Better to do things calmly and prudently. The saying is often associated with the fable of the rabbit and the turtle, where the latter manages to win by going slowly and without stopping.

Ride bene chi ride ultimo. – *Laughs best who laughs last.*

A temporary victory is not necessarily a definitive one.

Printed in Great Britain
by Amazon

79667792R00130